Life With "Father"

One man's journey into light…and love

Jacqueline A. Switzer

authorHOUSE®

AuthorHouse™
1663 Liberty Drive, Suite 200
Bloomington, IN 47403
www.authorhouse.com
Phone: 1-800-839-8640

© 2007 Jacqueline A. Switzer. All rights reserved.

No part of this book may be reproduced, stored in a retrieval system, or transmitted by any means without the written permission of the author.

First published by AuthorHouse 9/17/2007

ISBN: 978-1-4259-7815-0 (sc)

Library of Congress Control Number: 2007902545

Printed in the United States of America
Bloomington, Indiana

This book is printed on acid-free paper.

Dedication

To all my friends and colleagues who have supported me in my life adventures and professional endeavors. Most especially to my children who have encouraged me and loved me always, even through the crazy times. I thank you. And to you, Roger, the love of my life.

Introduction

The issue of priestly celibacy has been a topic of discussion in many sectors of the Catholic Church off and on for many years. Most recently it has surfaced again in relation to the incidents of pedophilia within our church. Forty years ago this was not the case. Questioning the need for mandatory celibacy or discussing the possibility of optional celibacy was the beginning of a ground-breaking dialogue.

The similarity between the two issues now and then is the response of the Church to both situations......... denial. Men who wanted to discuss the ramifications of the vow of celibacy and the compatibility to "real" life were restricted from doing so. A papal statement declared that it was not an appropriate topic for discussion. If there were any priests who had been released from the vow of celibacy, it was kept secret. It would seem that they were in some sort of "witness protection" program.

I am not a theologian or church scholar. I am a lifelong Catholic who has been faithful to the practice of my religion all my life. I attended Catholic schools from first grade through college; high school and college by choice. I taught Latin and religion for three years in a Catholic girls' high school. I declare openly that I received an excellent education and was fortunate to have some of the best instructors at all levels. It was because of the great example of these educators that I decided to become a teacher.

I was not accustomed to challenging the components of my faith. I have rarely been a visible activist for causes, but I openly and honestly contribute to dialogues and group discussions about important issues. Likewise, I try to keep informed about major issues within the church.

During my early years in Catholic school I recall learning certain precepts and mentally "questioning" the concepts, knowing well enough that I should not verbally "challenge" the idea. One such example was the teaching of limbo. I could not accept that the loving father, God, would relegate babies to a special place outside of heaven, if they were not baptized before they died. However I did not speak up.

I honestly did not give much consideration to celibacy. I knew many priests and worked with many religious and just assumed that the vows were taken as "acceptable" and necessary by those who were bound by them. As many students of Catholic schools, I gave some consideration after high school to entering the convent, however I knew that I would not be able to be obedient in all circumstances unless I understood and believed that the obedience was necessary. One of my senior advisors quickly suggested that perhaps I was not a viable candidate.

When I met and found myself in love with a priest, I became more educated in the aspects of celibacy and of course tried to learn all about the church's views on any possible changes. However as stated above the issue was shrouded in secrecy.

Roger was a pioneer in the struggle to allow priests to marry. He truly thought that the church would change the rule within ten years of our marriage. And here we are forty years later and no further along that path, but dealing with a tremendous shortage of priests and the issue of pedophiles.

The Church allows married protestant ministers who convert to Catholicism to become priests. The Church allows men who are divorced to become priests. The Church does not condone divorce, but will "annul" marriages that have produced children and have spanned many years. I sense in some of these issues a hint of hypocrisy.

In my early education about "vocations" I recall the list starting with religious, then married, then single...... somehow indicating a ranking order. And of course the very evident role of males in the ruling structure of parishes and the whole Church, somehow suggests a gender ranking order. We have made some progress in recent years so that women are now allowed to lector, give communion and direct parish business. However they cannot be ordained. I do not write this to rally for that change, only to point out the irony. It is interesting that convents have been more successful over the years in dealing with the shortage of vocations, than the priesthood has been.

The recent furor of the Catholic Church over the DaVinci Code and <u>stories</u> that Jesus may have had a relationship with a woman suggest to me that perhaps our institution does not hold women in high regard. It is my inclination to believe that this is part of the reason that the Church will not discuss the possibility of optional celibacy. And "optional" is what most people think is reasonable.

What follows is the story of one man who tried to follow the rules, request the release and marry in good favor with the Church. The emotional agony and the suffering are apparent as he struggled to accomplish this with little scandal to family, friends and Church. He did it with dignity.

Roger was a caring, loving individual. He taught me how to live, love and ultimately die with dignity. His life truly was one of service and love. One of my most profound memories of his last days is a time when we sat on the edge of the bed, he took my hand and said, "Jacq, I don't think I am going to win this one, but…… I have no regrets in my life." I was in awe…… what a way to come to the end…. No regrets!

This is one man's story……………..

Ordination and Graduation

I

For several days he had been saying *that there was something important that he had to say before we ended our work at the camp. And now, standing in front of me in the dining hall of the main building, he could wait no longer. "I think I am in love with you," he said. There was a long pause. He questioned, "Aren't you going to say anything?" And I said, "What do you want me to say? I love you, father." To which he replied, "Do you?" And I answered, "Yes."*

This brief intimate exchange triggered a year- long agonizing period of decision making. A young priest had to make a major decision about the priesthood and marriage, something considered mutually exclusive by the Roman Catholic Church. His dilemma; can I have both? And if not, which one do I choose?

On September 30, 1990 Roger Switzer, the Executive Director of the Charleston Housing Authority, my husband, and the father of our six children, stood before his colleagues, family and friends at the celebration of his health forced retirement. He spoke so eloquently and with heartfelt words about his work with the housing community. He remembered good times and difficult times. He thanked his colleagues for their help in assisting people of the community of Charleston with housing needs, jobs and real life issues. He asked forgiveness for times when he may have offended them or unintentionally caused hurt. Roger compared his work with the Housing Authority to the work of the priesthood, expressing his belief that it was far more encompassing than the active priesthood, which he left twenty-four years earlier. His audience heard this and understood the statement. However few knew the full story behind those words. That story has lain dormant for the last seventeen years since his death and now is mine to tell. It is the story of one priest's desire to marry, his agonizing discernment process, his attempt to conform to the church's requirements for laicization, and his life as a "married priest."

Switzer Children 1993 pictured left to right:
Andrew, Michael, Anne Marie, David, John and Richard

II

The journey begins....

In January 1965 I walked into the office of the Director for the Catholic Youth Organization in Rochester, New York to interview for a summer job at the diocesan camp. I was a (lay) Latin teacher at Our Lady of Mercy High School, my alma mater. Mercy High School was a Catholic girls' high school in Rochester, New York. It was staffed and directed by the Sisters of Mercy, whose motherhouse was adjacent to the high school. I had been teaching there for two years, and a fellow teacher had suggested to me that I might be interested in a job with the girls' encampment at Camp Stella Maris, a diocesan camp located on Conesus Lake. The Sisters of Mercy were non-counselor staff at the camp. The girls' session was three weeks during August, and my friend, Mary, had worked at Camp Stella Maris for several summers.

I expressed interest since this would fit well with my intended plans to attend summer school at Geneseo State College to study Spanish. Besides I was going to be staying with my parents who owned a cottage on Conesus Lake, not too far from the camp's location.

While I entered the interview thinking that I would be working as a counselor, with my colleague in charge, it soon became apparent that a director was needed for the girls' encampment, and I was interviewing for that position. I was hired. This was the beginning of my relationship with Roger Switzer.... Father Switzer.

During the following months I was engaged in interviewing trips to colleges and communities to hire a staff for the three-week girls' encampment. In March I received a letter from Father Switzer requesting an update on the progress of the "camp organization." He joked about the fact that his good friend, Father F., who was the chaplain at Mercy High School, had apparently not delivered any of his messages to me. He said he would be home for Easter and the week following and perhaps we could arrange a time to meet and go over details about staff. The letter closed: "You will be remembered in my Lenten prayers. I hope that you are managing to make it through Lent all right. Please give my best to Mary and Father F. (even though he didn't deliver my messages)." This was a pleasant, caring individual with a sense of humor.

Father Switzer was attending Catholic University to get a Masters of Social Work. He was ordained June 1959 and had been assigned as an assistant pastor at St. Mary's Parish in Horseheads, New York. In 1964 the diocese transferred him from there and assigned him as the director for the Catholic Youth Organization and sent him to Catholic University to study for a Masters in Community Organization.

In April 1965 while traveling to Florida for spring break, I stopped in Washington, DC to give Father Switzer an update on the hiring progress. Our visit was brief and he was very encouraging and cordial. During the subsequent months I completed the hiring process for staff for the girls' encampment.

In late June school was out for me, and Father Switzer had moved to the chaplain's cottage on the lakefront side at the camp, to get ready for the boys' encampment. Camp Stella Maris was a long-standing recreational retreat for the youth of the diocese of Rochester. Seminarians provided the staffing for the boys' encampment. Historically the seminarians cherished the camp experience during the summers of their study years and strong and lasting friendships developed during the summer experiences year after year.

During late June and July I stayed at my parents' place on Conesus Lake and attended Spanish classes daily at Geneseo State College. My parents' cottage was in the middle of the lake and when I was driving back from school, I had the option of going past the chaplain's place or going the other end of the lake. Frequently I would choose the former and if Fr. Switzer was at the chaplain's cottage, I would stop to visit. We mostly talked about camp business, but we had a chance to get to know one another better. He was a great conversationalist, had a wonderful sense of humor and was friendly and pleasant. Since I had been raised in Rochester and had attended Catholic schools there through college we had some mutual friends.

The camp was a 'refuge' for diocesan priests on their days off, and often at the times when I stopped by, someone might be visiting. Sometimes it was Fr. F., our chaplain at Mercy, whose dad worked at the same place as my father, and so we had great conversations about family, school, and of course church. This kind of visit remained the practice until the beginning of August. During this time I also met Fr. Switzer's parents, May and Earl, and his only surviving sibling, a brother Jerry. Jerry and his wife Annie and son Jimmy sometimes came to the lake for weekends.

Father Switzer

Fr. Switzer was the youngest of five children, four boys and a girl. The oldest son was killed in World War II, the next was killed in an automobile accident, and his sister died before Roger was born, at the age of 10 from leukemia. Roger's father was an only child and his mother was one of five children, one of whom was a priest in the diocese of Rochester. Roger was the care- taker of the family. He and his mom's brother Stewie collaborated to keep the peace as the family, or the "outfit" as they affectionately called it, dealt with numerous serious life and family issues. One very difficult issue was the struggle with alcoholism that the priest uncle faced for years.

Because of all the situations that Roger dealt with in his maturing years and during the time he was in seminary, he was viewed as very special in the family. And of course when a family had a member who was an ordained priest, they were viewed as special also. In the Switzer family Roger was a "saint," and "savior," because of all the issues that he helped the family face. His brother Jerry also struggled with alcoholism and struggled in his marriage and with his son. Everyone relied on Roger. This responsibility put added pressure on his decision making about the priesthood and his expressed feelings about me.

Not only was Fr. Switzer special in his family, he was also a special person to his fellow priests. He was a leader in the seminary, he was a confidant and he was the good humor man. The previous chaplain of Camp Stella Maris, who held the position for many years, was a quite different personality. So when Fr. Switzer took charge, the priests of the parish felt very welcome at the camp; the place that held such fond memories for them from their seminary summers. They felt comfortable and took advantage of the refuge that the serenity of the camp on the lake offered to them. Consequently there were many visitors on weekdays and on weekends.

By the end of July 1965, my classes were finished and we prepared for the beginning of the girls' encampment. The opening went smoothly and soon the routine of the activity schedule quickly engaged the staff. The job of the chaplain and the director became one of maintenance and monitoring. Frequently Fr. Switzer would come over in the afternoon and sit in my office and chat….. We were getting to know one another better. Often in the evening after the campfire and entertainment activities, when the campers were settled in their cabins, Fr. Switzer, any of his visitors and I would gather in the kitchen for coffee and fun conversation. He would joke a lot about my work and make cute comments to me. Years later Roger told me that after one such gathering when Fr. F. was visiting, Dave had said to him, "You have to be careful; Jacquie is the type of person that you could fall in love with." Roger said he didn't have the heart to tell him, that he was too late; it already happened.

By the end of the first week, his feelings had to be revealed. Once his love was proclaimed, the remainder of the encampment was clouded with the intensity of the meaning of that revelation, and the impact on our lives. Our conversations were different of course. We were guarded in our statements when others were present, not wanting to arouse any suspicion. When we were alone our words were drowned in the ponderous impact of the decision that Fr. Switzer had to make. We had admitted our love for one another and now we were trying to determine how that love could be fulfilled in a marriage commitment. We found some solace in the fact that we had time to consider all the ramifications of our proclaimed love. Fr. Switzer would return to Washington in September to complete his master's study, and I would return to teaching at Mercy High School.

During the final weeks of the encampment Fr. Switzer and I not only talked, we prayed. We prayed that God would help us with our decision, that He would guide us in the right direction. Roger shared that he had been thinking about celibacy a lot during the last year. He and his fellow students had had long discussions about the relevancy of celibacy to the priesthood and the possibility of the church allowing optional celibacy. Many of his colleagues had researched and were writing about the issue. He was saying that the groundwork had been laid and I had walked into the picture. He was now faced with the reality of the conversations, the research and the writing, and he was building the foundation for the possibility of being a married priest. On the lighter side, this was also the time when I became accustomed to calling him Roger instead of "Father" as we talked and shared. As a lifelong Catholic this was different. Indeed I did not even call my long time girlfriends who had entered the convent, by their given names.

On several occasions during this time I saw Fr. Switzer kneeling before the altar of God in the camp chapel. Here was a man in anguish. This was not a frivolous attraction, it was not about a sexual attraction; it was about a commitment and maintaining that commitment in a new dimension of life. It would have been easy to just walk away from the lives we had, and go off by ourselves to begin our new lives. But that was not Fr. Switzer. He was a man of integrity, a man who loved the priesthood, loved God, and now loved a woman and wanted to marry. But he was also a man with deep consideration for the ramifications of his decision on the lives of our families and friends.

In that respect, I thought that we needed to make my immediate family aware of our situation since I would be staying in Rochester and for a brief time would still be living in my parents' house. We "arranged" a meeting with my mom and dad at their cottage. Roger was somewhat reluctant because he did not know my parents well and did not know what they might think. I reassured him that my dad would be very practical; he would view Roger as a man who happened to be a priest. My dad was not a person to be swayed by position.

And so it was. We sat lakeside at my parents' cottage and Roger told them that he was in love with me. He said that we were going to find out how we could be married, and we would appreciate their support. My dad's comment? "Yep, you do have a problem." My mom had already made her contribution. A few weeks earlier while she and I were sitting by the lake, I asked her how someone would know when they were in love. Her reply? "I don't know, you just know it." My parents were supportive. My dad was always one to mind his own business and my relationship with my mom was more formal than emotional. So they were receptive and empathic when I shared, but not intrusive. I have three sisters and at that time the older one was married, and of the two younger ones, one was in college and the youngest was in elementary school.

As I thought that it was important to talk with my parents, Roger wanted me to meet with his lifelong friend and fellow priest, Charlie C. Charlie was teaching at Catholic University and frequently gave talks around the country. He was a well known and recognized, moral theologian. Roger had shared his "situation" with Charlie, who indicated that he wanted to speak with me. Priests were often the objects of "crushes," and Charlie wanted to find out for himself if this was the case with Roger and me. We met and he asked me many questions. This was not a crush.

Roger's long process of reconciling his love of God, of the priesthood and of a woman now began. He was on his way to Washington and I was back teaching school. The excerpts from the letters that Roger wrote to me daily unveil the emotion, the anguish and the hope that we experienced as he made his decision.

III

The longest road ......

September 22, 1965 – Today begins the time of separation which will enable us to measure our love. My conversations with Fr. C. today have not given me any other answers. Nothing is new. Please continue your fervent prayers for our intentions. The time today has really hung heavy. The only answer lies in our earnest prayers.

Fr. C. will have more answers on writing to Rome soon after we get to Washington. My head is whirling more than ever right now. I certainly hope that your parents will be a help to you these next few weeks.

September 23 - Back in D.C.

Today produced more talking and no decisions between Fr. C. and myself. At least it is good to have him nearby. At any rate I am back at the University ready to begin an 'important year.' God is good and He will help us in our love I am sure…… Let us continue to pray for each other.

September 24 - Our separation is some 48 hours old now, and it is very difficult. I sure hope that you are finding an outlet in your schoolwork. Please God that all will work out fine! My thoughts are certainly filled with ambivalent notions. It is no joke to be caught between two loves. Our love for one another is extremely strong. I have no doubt about this. My love for the priesthood is equally as strong. I have no doubts about this. The reconciliation of two loves is extremely tenuous though I am doing my very best to accomplish this. The "epic" goes on now amid different surroundings. You are especially in my thoughts and prayers as I realize how hard the struggle must be for you.

I would gladly suffer for both of us, yet I realize that this is an impossibility…..Next week I am going to the Trappist Monastery in Virginia to do a "little thinking." The following weekend, I will be home God willing. The ecstasy and agony routine has begun again for me.

September 27 - My happy moments have outweighed my unhappy moments lately. However, I do miss you terribly. Must be that I am in love with you. What do you know about that?

More and more I <u>know</u> that all will work out. The mountain may be steep, but then you and I are very persevering people n'est pas?...... God is so good. I know there must be a way for us. We will continue to keep on praying and planning because our love is true, and therefore, there has to be a <u>right</u> solution. You better believe it!

September 28 - I just came from the chapel. It was a pleasant chat with God. Today I feel quite happy and confident that all will work out well. Our prayers will be heard, I am sure. ...... In a way I can think more clearly here about what I must do about my status. Each day, it becomes more clearly defined in my own mind. I am less and less afraid to act on my decision (excuse me – our decision). It is helpful to realize that you still feel strongly about it. God will help us over the rough spots, I am <u>sure.</u>

(When we were talking together or on the phone, using the phrase "our decision" was a source of some minor debate. Roger would refer to "our decision" because he said that we were both in this together. I would say that it was his decision because I did not want to coerce him into leaving the priesthood to marry. I did not want him to think that I was forcing him to a decision. I wanted him to know that

I loved him enough to let him go……if that is what he decided. This was a difficult and some may think a silly definition of ideas. However it was important to us.)

September 29 - After work (his field experience) I went over to the National Shrine to pray and finish my breviary for the day. I assisted at the 5:15 Mass and prayed very deeply for our intention. I really felt good after Holy Mass……

It has been a happy type day in which I thought a lot about you and how much we love one another. This always makes me happy. ……I just <u>know</u> that we will find a solution to all of our "problems." Sorry about the word. Remember, I <u>really</u> <u>love</u> <u>you</u>! How fortunate I am to really have your love. It must be that I have done some good in life to deserve it or probably God is just that generous. …..

There is no doubt that we love one another very deeply, and there is no doubt that there has and will be a certain amount of suffering connected with this love ---this is life! It however is nice to <u>know</u> that <u>we shall overcome</u>. It is nice to feel your presence in what I do and in what I suffer, and it is nice to <u>know</u> that I am there beside you in your daily trials. And remember, I am suffering no more than what you are. And besides, it is all <u>really</u> worth it……

God keep you, and <u>thank you</u> so much for your love and concern. The clouds will pass- have no fear. Our love for one another and for God is too strong to be upset by mere human hindrances Right? …. God bless you and keep you as I send you all my love!

October 2 - I am learning to live with our separation, but it will be wonderful to see you on Saturday. There are a lot of things to be discussed. It is pleasing to hear that you are praying so hard. This will help us a lot. My own prayers of course are filled with happy intentions for you and me. ……

My adjustment to school is going along well. Thanks to your prayers. Things will fall into place gradually – then it will be easier to plan for our future. As I have said so many times, it will take a lot of planning. Soon, it will be getting to the stage where we will be able to do more joint planning, I hope. ……

Since I have returned, many of the "bull sessions" around here have centered around the law of celibacy. (I was more than an uninterested participant, needless to say).

(Initially Roger had a great deal of enthusiasm and optimism for a positive and affirming response from the Church hierarchy to his "situation." He was a trusting and caring individual and he thought sincerely that if you served well and were honest, you would be treated likewise in response.)

October 3 - Next weekend should be far different. I am looking forward to it. Father C. is back from St. Louis. He had a chance to talk to a few more people. Nothing looks very favorable at this writing. We are at present mulling over the idea of having Father C. write to Bishop C. in Rome. He will tell him the whole story keeping, of course, our anonymity. This could accomplish two things 1. The bishop could find out what could be done "ante factum" and 2. We could get the reaction of the Bishop to the whole thing. Besides the Bishop might think kindlier of the whole thing being "removed" from the acute physical presence of the problem. ....

Your letters are a constant source of encouragement to me. I really know how hard it is for you, and this makes me feel doubly sorry.

This morning I offered Mass "for us" and I served Father C.'s Mass as he too offered Mass for our intention. God will certainly give us the "right" answer as we have said right along. My thoughts are constantly occupied with "this matter of our love." My faith in prayer and my love of God has not been shaken to this day- nor will it be. What's more, I know this is the way you feel also. You are beautiful in all ways. You are generous, considerate, loving and understanding. All of which means you are especially "chosen" by God. He will not let you down nor will you let Him down, right? The days that lie ahead will most certainly not be easy. We will need every bit of spiritual strength we can bring to our disposal.

October 5 - Time and distance have really complicated matters. Right now, it is your faith and prayers that are keeping me going. Thank you! And I really mean it. It seems as if I am wandering in the "valley of death" - like Francis Thompson's "Hound of Heaven." This is the kind of mood I am in....In your own bright and cheery way, you lift me up. God grant me the courage that I need! I keep saying, "I love Jacquie and she loves me. Why does it have to be so difficult? Why are there so many obstacles?"......

You are so good; we are praying so hard. God help us. He <u>will</u>. He <u>is</u>....... Please forgive me for burdening you with these thoughts, but I just have to share them. (After Mass) things are better already. I really prayed hard at Mass. I am sure that God will give me the strength to do all the hard things I have to do.

October 6 – This has been a real hard week in so far as my moods have been concerned----just too much <u>thinking</u>. Through it all I <u>know</u> that I love you and I keep asking God to help me through these anxious moments. However, on the other side everything seems to be negative. Keep praying hard. What we do must be <u>right</u>. There can be no two ways about it.

You deserve only the best. I could give you <u>only</u> that. I could not give you half of myself. <u>This I know</u>. Our prayers will most certainly be answered. The mystery is how God can be so near and so far at the same time.

October 11 - Eternity + 12 hours…… (after a weekend at home) the sadness in my heart last evening has lasted to this moment. Your tears represent mine as well. Only God knows how much I love you – though you too have a pretty good idea. ….

Pray hard, my love. Our prayers will make our love an even greater reality. God will not allow this agony to go on much longer. He will give us the answer and the courage to accept it. I <u>strongly</u> <u>feel</u> that you are right. I know that there is still much thinking for me to do --- by myself……

Please forgive me for whatever sorrow I have caused you over the weekend. You know that hurting you is the farthest thought from my mind—if I still have a mind. …..

Our love is so good and so wholesome that it will have to come to fruition. I would be more than happy to take your sufferings as well as my own – unfortunately this is an impossibility.

Life with Father

I do hope you can see Father V.* real soon. He will be a help to you. We must believe that all our suffering will not be in vain.

* A fellow priest friend of Roger's, stationed in Rochester and the person with whom I chose to counsel. I was still living with my parents and Fr. V. was someone with whom I could share my thoughts, feelings and anxieties about our "situation." He could keep me balanced.

October 11 - the second - It has been a terribly long day, I have just returned from the airport. This time, I put Father C. and Father S. on a plane for Chicago. They are going to the Canon Law convention. I pray that Fr. C. comes back with some good news about our canonical situation.....

When I finish this letter I am going to chapel to spend an extra ½ hour before the Blessed Sacrament. Christ has always aided me in the past. I feel so completely empty without you! Today I have been in a complete fog.

(Later) God just isn't going to tap me on the shoulder. Agony still seems to be the chief character in our little epic. Knowing the torment I am going through makes me feel the more for the tortures you are going through. I know that the intensity cannot long remain because God is too good to allow this. He will have to give us the answer. Meanwhile, we have our love for one another.

How totally inadequate I feel at the present moment. I must fill my mind and heart with all the happy moments we have had together. The broken glass is too painful. The joy of our meeting on Friday is a help over some of the rougher spots of last weekend. How sorry I am for the sadness I have caused you. God Help me ---better still, God help us. I trust in our prayers – maybe even more than my own. At any rate, my prayers are our prayers and I know that your prayers are also our prayers.

What will keep me going these next few days is the knowledge of your love. <u>This I really feel</u>.

October 12 - I assisted at the 5:15 Mass after spending a half hour before the Blessed Sacrament. Our intention was given to God in the best way I know how. Knowing God's will is most difficult. (please see the enclosed newspaper clipping)* It would seem once again that everyone is on the other side.

Our judgment has to be a real sane and sober one in light of the obstacles against us. God will definitely give us the answer, as our love of him is great. Our own love for one another is likewise very great, as we both know. We have to be true to one another and to God at the same time. This is the difficulty. We must be sure never to hurt one another. Our love is so good; it must continue to remain that way. It is our fervent wish to sanctify this love in marriage. Please God that this may be possible.

God has given us the strength to this date, and He will continue to do so. My love of you has resanctified my life. Thank you! You have much to give to God. May I be in some way the instrument of your giving to God. This is what I hope for in one way or another. Hopefully, I also have some good to give to God. May you be the instrument of my gift to God!

Indeed, you have given me so much these last two months (eternities). I hope you have had a chance to talk to Fr. V. He can be such a consolation to you. I long to see you again, but this separation is necessary. Though I cannot explain it, I have always believed that no suffering properly accepted is in vain. Our acute and trying suffering likewise is no exception to the rule.

My doubts honestly expressed to you (even though they were the cause of tears) are part of my suffering. Your many anxieties are your suffering. Together, they make our suffering for our cause. I hope it is not boastful to say that we will not be wrong in our decision.

I am anxiously awaiting your letter to know your feelings since we parted early Monday morning. Truly we have known a wonderful love. How grateful I am to you for what you have given me.

*Pope Bans Open Debate of Celibacy Question

Vatican City…Oct. 11…..Pope Paul today banned any public discussion on the question of celibacy in the priesthood. The 2,142 prelates attending the Council are scheduled to begin debate later this week on a draft decree on the priestly life and ministry. The draft includes a strong reaffirmation of the traditional celibacy of the Roman Catholic clergy in the West.

Following the example of the Orthodox Church, however, some Easter Rite branches of the Roman Catholic Church allow priests to marry before their ordination. …….Pope Paul's decision was conveyed in a letter to the presiding Cardinal. The letter said that ……it was "not expedient" for such a delicate matter to be debated in public. The pontiff added that the practice of celibacy should be retained, but any prelate wishing to raise the issue could submit his views in writing and these would be brought to the Pope's personal attention.

By a vote of 2126 to 13 the Assembly today gave overall approval to a decree on how monks, nuns and other members of religious orders should adapt their lives and dress to modern conditions!!!

(The irony of this is so evident..... the Church will not adapt its policy on celibacy to "modern conditions," but the lives and dress should adapt.)

October 12 - How hard I am trying to make the right decision. I do not want to make the "easy" decision (and neither do you). In fact, no decision will ever be easy. So great is my love of you. You have given me such a wonderful gift – your love.

God has given me the priesthood. Everyday I say: quid retribuam Domino pro omnibus quae retribuit mihi? (What shall I give to God for all that He has given to me?)

This is quite a question. It deserves quite an answer. You and I have to come up with the answer. No one else can make it for us. Remember, it is our answer.

(Some of these thoughts indicate the agony of his decision. Roger wanted to make sure no one was hurt by his desire to marry. In fact he was really optimistic that he would be able to become a married priest, and if not that, then he could be relieved of his vows and then marry. As time went on he faced the realization that the Church was not going to be so accommodating….. no matter who the person was.)

October 14 - If you would rather that I didn't write, just let me know. Maybe you already have decided. However I thought that we agreed that it would have to be a mutual decision.

Strange: you were so sure from the beginning and I have been the up and down one. If you are sure the other way now, I am still up and down.

At this writing I guess I am more up than down. I know more than ever that I love you. This will never change. It will not be easy to "get over it " – nor do I ever really want to get over it. I want very much to marry you, but if this is impossible, then God will provide in another way. He will never take my love away – and that is good and wonderful – though it may be impossible to understand.

There are so many things that I do not understand anymore, though I continue to pray for light. Being human may have its rewards, but it also has its punishments.

I have never doubted God's love for me. Though sometimes, I find its manifestation difficult. Right now I find it extremely difficult. What way can I possibly make up for the hurt I have obviously caused you? How can I say that I am sorry that I fell in love with you? How can I say that I am sorry that I am still in love with you? Why can't I ask God not to allow me to love you? Yes, there are so many questions to be answered. I don't mean to be bitter, and I am trying hard not to be bitter. Please pray for me --- for us. You have given me so much. How can I ever thank you?

You worry me so much. At least when I heard from you, we were sharing our epic! Strange, but I have never lived on memories before. Is this what our lives are to be? Some reward for being good, huh? Sorry, but I am trying so hard not to be bitter!

One thing I am absolutely certain of is that you will always be my love and I am sure God doesn't mind this. God may have some ideas of how this is to be demonstrated. I keep asking Him to let me in on it. He <u>will</u>!

October 15 – Fr. C. returned from Chicago with a "radium" (ray of hope.) He found out at the Canon Law Convention by quietly asking people, that there are at least three "ante factum" (before the deed) cases pending before the Holy Office right now; two from Chicago and one from the West some place. This is the first ray of hope; remember I said God wouldn't let us down. Pray that these cases receive an affirmative response.

Today is our 2nd anniversary - eight weeks ago today at 1:45 p.m. I told you that I loved you. I meant it then and I mean it now. God grant that the happiest fulfillment will come of our love!.....

This separation is a good test – and the old saying that absence makes the heart grow fonder really has meaning!

October 16 – As I have already explained I have felt compelled to write to try to explain what was going on in my feeble little mind from day to day......I want <u>very, very</u> much to marry you. There is <u>some</u> reason to believe that this is possible. I am still praying that the possibility becomes <u>really</u> possible.

Objectively there is weight enough to believe and know that we can be right! Subjectively there is an even greater feeling that we are right.

This is a very human situation...... I keep praying for us. Each day I feel more and more that we are committed to one another at all costs. There is no "easy" way out, my love.

October 20 - My concern for your ability to "weather the storm" is still paramount. So, please be honest on Saturday about how things are really going. My faith in our continued good judgment has been strengthened by our phone conversation......

In spite of all the thinking and praying this week things have been fairly happy, happy- which I know will please you. I keep praying that this is not all too much for you – such an epic!

October 25 – I am sorry that I could not have been more definite about many things – but now I know that you really understand the situation as far as I am concerned. This makes me love you all the more! Because ----you are so patient.......

My thoughts and worries are less burdensome in a way – just knowing that you are so good and so understanding. Certainly I am trying hard to really make up my mind and you know that.

There is no doubt that our love for one another has given us both a new dimension in life. This is wonderful with all its implications. In this sense, one can live on love.

October 26 - This week I am in a state of philosophizing – a new mood. I am definitely trying to be more "objective" about our love – don't think trying to be objective isn't quite a philosophical problem.

You are so good to bear with me. I find it hard to bear with myself.

Everyone has always thought me to be so stable – the rock- the solid type par excellence. This is the way I have always functioned. And then a little butterfly attacked my turtle shell. And here I am – with you flitting all over my mind.......

The same old question – I have a real love for you and you have a real love for me. This is a fact. Next question – quid faciendum? (what can be done) the answer is still not completely evident. What I must do has to be right. What I want to do might not be right. Being good is a good thing. Being human is another good thing. Being good and human at the same time is a difficult thing. Please keep praying. Remember, I am relying on the help of your prayers, also.

Brief visit in Rochester for the weekend.

November 3 – I felt much better after "our talks" over the weekend. I am less worried over you because of your assurance that you could survive. God is good, and He will give us the strength.......

You are right about me staying here to Thanksgiving- I guess it is best! Thank Fr. V. for me when you see him, won't you ?.......

Life with Father

God bless you and keep you as I send you all my love.

November 4 - You are right. Your letter cheered me immensely. It seems that we have passed another critical milestone in the Epic. Though it is hard to understand, it will all have been worth it......

Please stay happy. Keep trying. We have a difficult road to travel, but sincerely all things are possible and good to those who love God---you already know this.

Fr. V. is at your disposal for "conferences" anytime. This is a help and a consolation.

November 5 – Your letters seem quite happy. You are so good to suffer in silence – but it will be worth it, and our prayers will be answered I am sure. It seems like we repeat things, but certainly some things are worth repeating – like l love you!

November 6 – The tone of your letter was somewhat depressing. I am sorry about the home situation. However, it would seem that this is another part of the suffering and anxiety connected with our love. You must grow in the midst of this misunderstanding. It will be difficult – and this is where prayer and patience comes in. Your next visit with Fr. V. will certainly help relieve some of the tension.

Keep your chin up- pray hard; place your trust in Christ who knows our human nature better than anyone else. If we are true to Him, we cannot lose! The months that lie ahead will have their sadness as well as happiness- at times it may appear that they will have more of the former than the latter. Hang on, Sloopy!

I haven't heard anything new from the Chicago situation yet, but a few things have happened around here that have given me greater hope. I'll explain later.

November 8 – News from home hasn't been the most pleasant lately, but I guess things will work out there! This week I hope to do a little investigating about jobs here in the Washington area. Even if plans are to be long range, I guess they have to be considered. Huh?

I've had a few talks with Fr. C. lately – nothing new or important to report in that regard……

Like yourself I have felt more like "me" lately. Actually I take this as a sign that we have passed a major milestone in our epic. What do you think?

November 10 - I'll be going to 5:15 Mass at the Shrine. You will be <u>especially</u> remembered in my prayers. God is our best friend- and it's a good thing He is. Our "case" certainly is special and will require "special" attention. I hope you get a chance to see Fr. V. before too long. You are always especially happy after talking to him.......

Remember I love you very much. There just has to be an <u>ultimate</u> <u>happy</u> solution to our love. Time will help us work this out – for a happy, happy ending, huh?

November 11 -......This has just got to work out. I love you so much – it isn't funny! My mind is worn out trying to think of all the possibilities. There doesn't seem to be much "ecclesiastical reason" for hope though. This is the major difficulty.

It really was a big disappointment to find out that there was nothing to the "Chicago story" at all. Now, temporarily, I am without a plan. Pray hard that something will break in this direction.

To go off without any "benediction" is going to be a truly hard decision – for both of us. It will take much prayer, huh? Sorry, to inject this "realism" but we must think of these things, unpleasant as they may seem.

Your last letter sounded real enthusiastic. Your love of teaching is a real consolation.....

Please God we must be successful. Talk about the dark night of the soul! The Northeast power failure is a nothing compared to the darkness of life without you.

November 13 –Your letter of Wednesday I have just read twice. Your anguish is clearly expressed, and it is very much the same as mine. This is the "agony and the ecstasy" of it all. It is a strange fate that has "thrown" us together, and somewhere in it all is God who is <u>all good</u> and <u>all</u> loving. "Magnum Mysterium......."

You know very much that I love you with all my heart. I can't help it; it is a fact. The "Problem" is how my love of you will be realized and fulfilled. You know my hopes, desires, prayers and wishes. Being "human" certainly has its harder moments. All I can continue to say is that we must pray, love God and hope. I am doing all that I can humanly do to make everything right!

Fr. V. writes: "How are you doing? I'm prayin' Rog, just for light and courage for you. Some how Rog, I'm tremendously confident that in the long run you'll be square, true, and loving to God, yourself, Jacquie and people."

A tall order – a trememdous confidence. God grant that everyone's prayers are answered. No one seems to know the <u>whole</u> answer. The thought of "losing" you is equally depressing for me.

Honestly, outside of my love of God, I have never known a love like yours. God does not reciprocate in "human" terms. But by the same "logic of love" God has never let me down. He is <u>real</u>- like <u>people</u> <u>type</u> real.

The 'tiredness' that you spoke of is felt by me. It is the result of this conscious and unconscious wrestling with "our love problem." The accent is on love – not on the problem – though the tiredness comes from the problem – not from the love. ....

We will do the right thing. We must not let God down. This is all that I can say. Each step has to be carefully considered. Our love is good; it is real; it is wonderful; <u>it</u> <u>is</u> <u>a</u> <u>mystery.</u> God must help us solve the mystery.

How it hurts me to see you tortured by this! For I really feel your agony. That is why I know it is love. How wonderful is this love – how fearful is this love! God be good to US. ....

I hope what I write doesn't further confuse you, but rather I hope that it helps you to understand how much I really love you........

Does the mountain seem higher than it did a few weeks ago? Maybe it is—maybe it isn't. But it is there, huh? Hand in hand, heart in heart, we have begun the ascent. As we look back the view is only beautiful. As we look ahead, it can only be beautiful.

November 14 - ……Your letter of yesterday really "shook me up." How hard it is for you. How strange a world we live in that we should both suffer so much --- just because we are in love! Again, "magnum mysterium."

We just have to keep praying and hoping – the sun has to shine again. Our suffering will certainly be rewarded…..

God will be good to us. You must continue to have faith in this fact. I know that you do. Your love of God is strong… one of the reasons I love you so much. <u>Ours</u> is certainly the greater love for all of this.

November 16 - I am working real hard trying to figure everything out –trying to make plans as best I can – all because I love you so much. A lot has happened to me in this last million years. You have added so much to my life – now I really am "Jolly Roger."

Still much sorrow and many trials lie ahead but our prayers will help us I am sure. Because I love you so, I don't want to see you hurt in any way whatsoever. But can this really be? What we need most of all is a miracle! If our love is a miracle, maybe we can come up with another one, huh? ……. (comments and questions about time we can spend over the Thanksgiving holiday) ……Keep happy and keep on praying hard- who knows – maybe we will have a miracle? You're the girl who can cause one, I am sure. You're my own little miracle worker – just you believe it.

November 20 - …. Because we love one another, we must do what is best for each of US and both of US combined. This, my love, is what makes me vacillate so much. Only complete honesty with one another and with God can lead us to happiness together. Yes, this is my hope and wish. This is what I pray for daily – even hourly. I am sure you understand this, and I am sure you understand how much I love you. It would be impossible for me to go through the mental torment of it all if I did not love you so much.

Yes, there are <u>two</u> easy ways out right now. One would be to run away <u>from</u> you. And the second would be to run away <u>with</u> you? I'd choose the second rather than the first, but right now I must choose neither – that's why we have to wait – cruel though it may seem.

Has not our love grown even from the beginning? Have we not grown in it? You are the only love other than God that I have ever known. My love of God, however, likewise has always been real and honest – though a bit confused at times. It has always been genuine – Thank God, this is the only way I can love…….

This is the only kind of love which you deserve. And please God, someday you may have <u>all</u> my love. Only with and through God's help will this be possible! I am sure you realize this more than ever now.

Fr. C. agrees this "can" be possible. This is our hope. This is what we have to build on. I know that I am repeating myself again, but it is only because I want you to so understand.........

Only prayer, honesty and a real look at ourselves will give us the answer. This "waiting" is to be sure of the truth. ....Our relationship has been so beautiful so far, and with the help of God, it will always be that way!

November 21 - You can be sure that I'll never love anyone as I love you. Furthermore, you can be sure that I have never loved anyone as I love you. Please God that we can make our love be a reality in marriage.

There are so many apparent obstacles, which cannot be wished away. God will give us the answer, huh – over a period of time and prayer. Here I am repeating myself again......

We have every confidence in one another – and this is good because this confidence is based on our love of God as well as our love of one another.

November 22 - We have much to discuss and I hope we can do it without the bitterness of last time. There are a couple of premises that we have to start off with

– You and I love God, and you and I love one another. Let's remember these premises and base all of our conversations on them, please!

There are so many things that indicate that both of these premises are true. Conclusions must be based upon them – right?

Prayer, time and honesty are our watchwords – they must be.

(Home for Thanksgiving holiday – these visits were wonderful, but not the ordinary that a couple would enjoy. We could not "appear in public." We could not go to one another's homes. We had to meet somewhere and talk in the car. Occasionally we might meet for lunch and Roger would have his collar on and if we met anyone who knew him (as we did once), they usually supposed that we were planning camp business or just meeting as friends since we had worked together at Stella Maris.)

November 29 – You are right – this stretch won't be as long as the last time and since many things have already been worked out, we might see the silver lining in the clouds yet. It ought to be beautiful – judging from the clouds we have seen......

Taking these hills one at a time is an easier way of climbing the mountain!...

I want to tell you that I am more confident all the while that our love will have a happy, happy ending! Yet there are a lot of prayers to be said, decisions to be made etc. And I suppose, some "serious" talk will be in order at Christmas time. We will have plenty of time.

November 30 - …..Please stay happy… we can work all this out with God's help, our own honesty and a will to do what is best for US…

(By this time Roger had shared some of the "situation" with a couple of his fellow priests at school. One in particular, Fr. S. stated that he was not in favor of what Roger was wanting to do, but he regarded Roger like a brother and would do anything he could to help him.)

December 2 – I really feel happy about our love, and it is a lot easier at school now. Your positive thinking really helps…..

Things are beginning to work out in a most wonderful way. Soon I'll be able to explain – just two short weeks. I am more sure than ever that God will provide us the way …..

December 4 – This time away from you is difficult, but it is not as hard as the last time, which means that

God is giving me the strength to bear the separation. As I mentioned before, a few very positive things have happened lately to give me greater hope. The mountain top doesn't look as high as it did a few months ago.

December 6 – I am truly sorry about being so cryptic in the last few letters, but I do not want to explain in a letter or over the phone – but it is good – like you! Yes, I have decided to talk to the Bishop at Christmas time, but I'll explain about this when I get home...... Please do not worry about what I am going to do. It will be all right, and it is the right thing to do...

All is well here and you sounded very happy, happy over the phone last evening. At Christmas time maybe we will be able to make some more definite plans for our future. I sure hope so!

December 8 – It is necessary that I talk to the Bishop at this time. There is no good reason to put it off any longer. Only good can come of our conversation – that is looking at it positively.

There are many things which you and I have to discuss together before I talk to the Bishop, and this can be done easier by us now – i.e. easier than it could have been done a couple of months ago. God is good, and He will continue to give us the strength we need for the days that lie ahead.

I hope that you feel that this is a proper time to begin with the ecclesiastical business. You have suffered through a great deal already.... All I can say is that this decision to talk to the Bishop makes me feel happier, and in turn I hope that it makes you happier.

We have come a long way, and there yet remains a distance up the mountain. The air seems to be getting a little thinner at this point, but my love of you is getting all the stronger.

I thank you for your love and the trust you put in my judgment, and I return the love and the confidence in you. Keep up your prayers.

There are many aspects of my present decision that I will talk over with you when I get home on Friday.

December 9 - Please God that all our dreams may come true! Even trying to think positively, there seems to be a tremendous about of obstacles. However, we must keep praying.....

You sound so happy in your letters and you sounded so happy over the phone! Why can it be wrong for us to want this happiness? Please God! ...

I don't want the way to be easy – I just want it to be right!

And I guess all the anxiety means that it is not going to be easy. But Please God, it must be right! ….

I have made up my mind to present my case to the Bishop. This will be another step in the right direction.

Maybe we will get our miracle! So, I better stop being so sullen, huh? But I must share even these depressing moments with you, my love. The love that I feel for you is real, and it will never pass, I am sure……

I am determined to have a miracle, O.K! How's that for being positive? Hang on Sloopy! I talked to my Mom yesterday, and things are well at home. Thank God for that…… Thank you for your love, your patience, and your understanding.

December 11 – I am terribly sorry about the pessimistic tone of that last letter. I was just depressed. You know how much I love you and how much I want to marry you with God's benediction. You know also that neither of us would be happy for long without God being on our side.

We have tried; we have prayed and there is a possibility that God will hear our prayers in the way we want them heard…….

On Monday morning I have an appointment with Cardinal Shehan of Baltimore to discuss this matter. The Cardinal just returned from the Council and he has graciously consented to see me. My prayers over the weekend are that he will be able to give us some hope. After all, he is pretty close "to the throne." Please God, there will be some happy answers to my questions.

I am sure that he won't be able to say anything definitive, but at least he can tell us what our possibilities are! ....

The fact that I am able to have this appointment has brightened my outlook..........

How often I am tempted to become bitter because there are so many interferences, but I must not be bitter and, my love, you must not be bitter either. Your goodness and capacity to love must give you hope – the truly Christian virtue!

There is naturally a certain amount of passion with our love. We must not be blinded by this- this is easier said than done.

It could be that God will reward us tangibly for the anxiety we have endured. I know that God will not let us down. We must not let Him down!

Each day I love you more and more! This is what makes it all seem so right! I want to tell the whole world ---"World, I am in love with Jacquie!" And like yourself, I am willing to sacrifice, if it will only come true!

December 12 - Tomorrow will be another big day in our lives. Please God my talk with the Cardinal is a fruitful one. So much depends on the conference. I am about ready for the part of this ascent up "our mountain." I know that you are here with me……. Needless to say I have a few "flutter bys" (he used to invert phrases and words) in my stomach at this stage. …….

I really love you and I long so to be able to marry you. I hope it will be in the Church! So hang on "Sloopy." It is so easy and natural for me to say that I love you, and that I want always to be with you. We have been so good and so considerate of other people. God must be on our side…….

Your letters sound wonderful, and I know how hard you are trying and I know how hard you are suffering in all of this. You are made of pretty strong stuff……

This has turned out to be quite a love story…… agonizingly beautiful. Our love has to be all the stronger for what we have been and will have to go through.

December 13 - My meeting with Cardinal Shehan was very discouraging; I'll explain more when I see you in person…. Pray hard for us…….

Your letter today helped the situation a great deal. You are so wonderful and so good. Please stay happy until I see you on Friday.

(Essentially the result of his visit to the Cardinal was that there probably was no hope for an ante factum (before the deed) decision from the Church.)

December 14 - Yesterday's meeting with Cardinal Shehan has still left its discouraging pallor with me. I have tumbled from heights sublime to ….. By the time you have received this letter, you will have talked to me over the phone, and you will have more details.

If not, I'll explain all when I see you on Friday. It seems as if we are back where we started four months ago --- only this time we are more in love. The irony of it all is perfectly terrible!

Only God can help us, my sweet, and this too will not be a pleasant help to endure… but more of that when I see you in person.….. I can hardly wait to see you though our meeting will be touched with a tremendous sorrow most unavoidably. God knows how much I love you, how much you love me.

And God will be good to us.….. You and I must never doubt this for our love has been built on this from the very beginning.

(Home for the Christmas holiday- the times when Roger was home and when we had a chance to see one another, our conversations were intense, agonizing and yet sometimes very happy.)

January 4 – Fr. C. just left my room a few minutes ago. We had a very pleasant discussion. He said, "It kind of looks like your mind is made up." Says I, "Yep, it is!"

It was a very pleasant vacation for me and I hope it was for you. Keep praying hard that I settle right down to business. Somehow, I feel that I really will now.......

I feel "sounder" than the last time I returned to school. How about that? It must be your prayers.

January 5 – It happened already – my first period of depression, but thank God, it was short.........

I am going to confession when I finish writing this letter. This always helps. And I am sure of your love; this is another help. God bless you --- but you sure got a bargain and a half when you met up with me – Droopy himself!..........

Jacquie, I know that you love me very deeply, and I know that I have caused you a great deal of anxiety by my doubtful attitude. I am terribly sorry for all of this – and <u>please</u> realize that it is all because I <u>never</u> want to hurt you.......

I really love you, Jacquie in spite of all my ups and downs. And, please God, we may begin to see more ups than downs in the New Year. You are so patient with me.

January 6 – When I returned from field work just now, your welcome letter was waiting for me. You are right about the separation being easier this time – for our love is that much more real. I love you truly, my love, and I could never hurt you, myself, or God, and so it remains to work out our destiny. God will not be wanting and I thank Him that He has used me as an instrument to make you happy – and bring you back to being your wonderful self.

You have much to give and much to share and God will show you and me the way. What we have given one another is an assurance that we can really be loved as well as really love. There has come to my mind again the ever haunting thought that God wants us to experience this love in a way not easy to bear at first. Only time and our own honesty will tell because it is quite evident that we know how to love – one another – our parents, relatives, friends and <u>God.</u>

Now is the time for earnest prayer and reflection. God has been so good to us. What is He asking in return? ….only you and I can tell. Such is our love for one another that we must tell the truth.

If I should have to give up the idea of marriage to you, it will be undoubtedly the hardest thing that I have ever had to do. For it will be like giving up part of myself-it will be like giving up all of myself! Please God, I will do the right thing.

I have known you so intimately, and I have been closer to you than anyone in my whole life. How I have longed to give you all of my love. Time and circumstances have held this gift in check. God knows best!

I do not write these things to make you feel sorrowful. I write them to demonstrate the wholehearted love that I have for you. Again I say I have been closer to you than to anyone else in my whole life – except God.

Our love for one another – in the prime of our lives is a genuine and real love. Should it demand the price of our separation, I am more sure now than I was before – we will be able to pay the cost. If – to think positively- we are able to be married, then likewise we will be able to pay the cost.

My thoughts are not morbid, but they are genuinely real. In the very beginning- when our love was young, we <u>promised</u> one another that we would not hurt each other and that we would not run from God.

Our love has grown, matured and yet a decision still lies before us. Much prayer and consideration of one another is necessary. I know now that you will stand by the decision that I must make (regardless of what it is) because you love me deeply. And likewise I know that I will make the best decision possible because I love you ever so deeply with every fiber of my being. And so it is in the <u>calmness</u> of our love that I will be thinking. Yes, my love, I will be able to work these three weeks because I am bolstered by your love. Thank you for this wonderful sympathy.

It is nice to know that two people can love so much and so tenderly – and it is especially nice to know that we are the two people.

I hope that you will be able to assist at daily Mass again for our intentions. We need help and strength from God. He alone knows, besides ourselves how much we love one another.

It is He who holds my love in check. …. Pray hard that we will do the right thing for each other, <u>for</u> <u>God</u> and for everyone. ………I am continually happy in your love for I know how unselfish it really is.

January 7 – I have a great feeling of peace that all will work out someway or another. This is really a peace – not just a passing feeling I hope. ……. and I just know that we will never do anything that is wrong. Our decision (or mine, if you prefer) will be right whatever it is, and God will grant us all the strength necessary.

On the positive side, I wrote to the Oriental Bishop of Philadelphia seeking some information (perhaps there is hope in this direction).

January 9 – Mea culpa, mea culpa, mea maxima culpa …. I really am sorry for the last few letters…it is nothing more than a delayed reaction… and it was very selfish on my part. Please forgive me.

I love you very much and I am willing to make all the sacrifices necessary to prove this love. Further I am aware of all the suffering this will likewise entail for you and I admire your courage to suffer more silently than I.

January 11 - …….Everything is going along fine and I am trying not to worry too much but let's face it, there are many things to be considered. …. Please don't worry about me – thanks to your prayers and love, I am keeping my head about things. ……Your love is keeping me going – there is not much else that you can do for the present except to listen.

January 14 - All sorts of plans are racing through my feeble little brain – and formulations are beginning to come. We will have much to discuss when I get home. What does the song say? "We can work it out." Yep, we can! Even though it may take some time.

January 16 – Everything is fine at this end – and I am managing to control my worrying quite a bit. Actually, I have been able to get a lot of work done. This afternoon I am typing the final draft of my third thesis chapter. …..When I do think of what lies before us, my darling, I do get a little frightened. This, I suppose, is a NORMAL reaction. Funny thing – these normal reactions. Knowing your love of me helps a great deal. Lately, I have been doing my very, very best to think positively. This also helps…. I love you, Jacquie, and I want so much to have all of your love in marriage. Please God that this dream will become a reality.

January 17 – Now what? When I didn't receive a letter on Saturday, I thought the mail was perhaps mixed up. When I didn't receive a letter this morning, I began to wonder…. I am trying very hard, my sweet, to do what is right – no matter how difficult it is! Lately I've been working real hard and getting a great deal accomplished. ….. And I know that this is all terribly hard for you! Do you feel that I am weak? Are you not writing for my sake? Do you feel that we are wrong? Jacquie, my sweet, I love you and I am trying my very best to show this in every way. I did ask you not to just stop writing when I had no idea of the reason why. Is it my fault? Are you afraid? IF so, welcome to the club! But we can't solve anything this way. Are you trying to tell me that we ought to try not to write? Do you think this is what I really want?

January 17 - #2 – I realize full well that there are a lot of things to be talked over when I come home, and that's why I hope to have a week or so. ...... And I am hoping and praying that when I talk to my parents everything will go smoothly. This will mean that many other plans can be made (first discussed) more quickly.... I am glad that you are so happy, and we will certainly be able to work out our many problems together. That's the main thing – and with that, we have a lot going for US.

January 20 – 5 months – anniversary of our proclamation of love.

This afternoon I did some reading – a very interesting book, "Priestly Celibacy and Maturity." There are a lot of wonderful ideas in it – there are also a lot of arguments for married priests. Maybe some day there will be

married priests in the Western Church. I hope so....
These past couple of weeks have been very productive for me in many ways. I am happy and thankful that my mind has been so at ease. God is helping a great deal – and I am trying to help myself with <u>your</u> love and strength very much in mind. You are a <u>real</u> help, 'ya know – and I mean it.

January 23 – I have been a little bit preoccupied with the thought of telling my parents at the end of the week. Thanks for the prayers and encouragement – it is a big help. This will be the hardest step to date, but your love and our prayers will really help a great deal. I haven't been morose about it, but it has bothered me considerably ......Maybe after this next hurdle, the second semester won't be so long. There are so many plans to be made!

January 24 – I've tried very hard not to baby myself but this business of telling my parents is tremendously difficult – because of their age and all the factors which I have already mentioned to you. Yes, I am trying to be objective, and I know my own parents better (obviously) than I know your parents – so it makes the situation that much more difficult, my sweet. I too have learned from you and I want you very much to help me and be my complement. You definitely have the ability to do so – but you could be much more vocal about it. If you really love me (and you do) then there is no need to worry about my reaction. We are, after all, not trying to trap one another. I believe this has already happened. What is happening now is that we are trying to grow in our love for one another. Honey, I don't want you to make decisions which I have to make – but I do want you to be a part of these decisions. I do want to know your feelings – good, bad and indifferent. We cannot hide these things! We have to learn to trust one another – silly as this may sound! ....

You are a part of me now, and I must know and feel your every thought and emotion just as you must do the same for me. This is love – no secrets. That's why I tell you exactly how I feel and why I think I feel this way at such and such a time. Sorry – my sweet- but this is I. If you love me (and I know you do) you have to love this part of me – and you have to try to understand it. You have the capacity to do so.

This is not to say that you have not demonstrated a great amount of love to this date, but there is much more that you are capable of – this is why I love you so – and I will not be content until I draw all of this out. And you must not be content until you drain me – for I must become you and you must become me.

Nor is this a cat and mouse game. You must possess me completely and I must possess you completely; even physical union is but a sign of this total personal union…..

I am trying so hard to make you a part of me. I know that I have succeeded a great deal, but there is yet more to do. Please be patient. … You are a spitfire by temperament--- and yet you fear to express this to me sometimes. Why ?

January 25 - ….. Maybe I am just too much of a baby, but maybe not also! I love YOU very much. And I am trying so hard to overcome a great many obstacles which I try to see and talk about…. And I am sometimes silent hoping that you will add to the conversation. After all it is OUR life and you are part of it. Please… let's talk sensibly when I come home. Don't be afraid, huh! If my concerns seem to be selfish, I am sorry – they really aren't. It is all important that I make a sensible adjustment for you know by now that I am a very sensitive person (and so are you), and therefore it is important to be satisfied with one's judgments………..

I spoke hurriedly once ……. and it caused quite a bit of turmoil afterwards- right! That's why I am more deliberate right now- trying to take my time – even though there appears to be a June deadline of some sort. You know that I am not playing with your emotions any more than I am playing with my own. I just don't operate that way. ….. My mind is fairly well made up – but there are steps in the process – talking to my parents and your parents again – these have a bearing. My love of you means wanting to make you very, very happy for the rest of your life. This takes quite a bit of considering. I would never want to hurt you in any way, and I am trying at all costs to proceed on this promise. It is a bit painful – now and again – but it will have a lasting value.

It is always <u>your</u> best interests that I have in mind – apparently I don't always make this clear and for this I am sorry. I love everything about you very, very much and this to me is a great joy, and I hope that it is a great joy to you……

My so called "moods" are occasioned by my determination to do things well. Perhaps you have a greater facility to manage "these weightier problems" or perhaps you try to keep too much to yourself.

Well – so much for the preaching. Remember, I love you so much it hurts. And I am sure it will work out all right – but there are going to be rough times ahead – and I want you to be fully aware of them.

(A Visit to Rochester – this was his semester break. By this time I was living with three other girls in a house we were renting. One of the girls (M) was teaching with me at Mercy High School. She had been dating a young man who had left the seminary several years previously. I shared our "situation" with my housemates. They had many questions and were guardedly supportive. When Roger was at home this time, he came over to visit. On one particular Sunday evening, we all played cards as we watched the snow accumulate outside. One of the girls was in Syracuse, skiing. This was a good thing because we were "snowed" in and Roger did not get to leave until the next day. This gave the girls a chance to get to know him and to ask all the questions they wanted.)

February 6 – What we have been through so far is a real sign of our love. What we yet have to go through yet will be an even greater sign… And we are both equal to it! But we have to take things day by day and not all at once…. We are growing in our love and in our happiness and this is what is important! God bless you.

February 7 – Our "situation" is still a difficult one and the separation doesn't help, but eventually the time will pass. Our prayers and efforts to do what is right will likewise be a help…..In the very beginning you said that you would be willing to wait an even much longer time.

Life with Father

God will give us the strength and He will help us to do the little things to make this bearable for <u>others</u>...... I know how hard it is for you – not to be able to share the joy and excitement of our love with others. At least you have your Mom and Dad and sisters --- And Fr. V. And as time goes on – perhaps the list will be tactfully added to!

February 8 – (Interesting note from his field experience in Silver Spring Maryland. An omen of his future career, perhaps.) This afternoon I am attending a meeting on emergency housing for poor people. One of the protestant churches in this county started a non-profit organization to help in this problem area. They are doing a fine job and it is a wonderful relevant idea for social action under a church auspice....... This evening Fr. C., Fr, S. and Fr. M. and I are going to take one of our Rochester visitors out to dinner.......After dinner we had quite a theological "bull session" – everything from original sin to dating morals.

February 9 - Our "epic" is about six months old (young) now. We have come a long way – with more ecstasy than agony, I believe. So here's hoping and praying.

Jacqueline A. Switzer

February 10 – Yes, we'll have to talk to your parents when I come home again. You said that your Mom was surprised that I was going to be working in Rochester next year. You can tell her not to worry about scandal – we've done pretty well so far – at least I hope we have….. My prayers and thoughts are aimed at asking God's help to develop the necessary "patience and endurance" – or "stubbornness" if you will.

February 12 – Fr. C stopped in last night and we had quite a visit. We discussed our (i.e. Roger's and mine) plan to wait a year after graduation. He seemed to agree that this sounded sensible in view of the fact of finances, adjustments etc. He knows what a problem it will be to explain to my parents. I told him of your visit to my house, and he thought that was a good idea. We discussed the fact that it was hard on you to wait, but I said that you were agreeable. At any rate, he agrees that June would be pushing everything too much. He wanted to know how you were reacting to all of this and I tried to explain your feelings in the matter. Perhaps when you are down here, we can talk to him a bit.

The following "poem" was Roger's way of "venting" and narrating the love, the frustration, the agony of our situation…reviewing our experiences of the past four months.

"Though the verse may be blank, the love is real."

Eternity almost captured in four months' time

A love ever so tender, almost mine!

A potion so sweet, never to be drunk

A vision of beautiful humanity overshadowed by a sorrowful but truthful Divinity.

My feet of clay upon a blitheful, mirthful path of love trod.

Torrentially my life's stream cascaded happy, happy, happy.

And my eyes twinkled because they beheld a reality called love.

Honestly, hopefully, happily – though haltingly the climb was begun.

"You don't make such a climb with everyone."

A tear filled note, a happy ride, a long walk, a laugh, an agonizing hour of payer, a smile, an embrace, a boat, a bench, a lake, a swing, Niagra's wonder, leafless Mount Vernon, a snowy route 33.….

Hand in hand, heart in heart, time would tell; the world would see a love so true! August became December, and in a lofty building, I stood before a Prince of our Church, a prelate close to the Vicar of our God.

NO – never echoed so soundly, a shattering blow….
Tears furrowed my soul while their inconsequential

counterpart trickled down a face that previously had known no greater sadness.

God is a jealous lover… what is His is His only…Is it consolation to be allowed in the garden of olives to whisper Christ's very own prayer, "Not my will be done, but Thine"….only time will tell.

Job's dunghill is like a palace to me now.

For I am more than homeless and naked…

Flesh that would have been my flesh has been it seems, ripped unmercifully from my vibrant manhood.

My heart barely murmurs – for its mate is untimely snatched away..

"God will provide" are ice-incased words to be melted only by the reality of wanting Him … time will tell.

Would that I could give you the world. And I cannot even give you myself for I belong to Another.

Our love must be in, through and with Him Who is love… should it always be at a distance, it will always be real - for I can love in no other way….. Next to God, Jacquie, I love you.

May He reward US and sustain US… I have scarcely strenth to say… only time will tell of God's pleasure with the oblation which I give Him today – myself.

Life with Father

Should He return me, I am yours. Should He keep me for Himself, I am still yours.... In Him ... forever.........Roger.

February 24 ....(Roger is making a retreat) The retreat is going well. This afternoon and this evening we discussed and will discuss priestly celibacy. More about that later... I love you very, very much and I am trying to grow even more in that love. Always I want to do what is best for you. That is why time is necessary. There are so many realities to be considered. We shall overcome, I am sure, but not overnight and not without a lot of blood, sweat and tears. This is the price we will have to pay, and we must ready ourselves to pay the price. My love of you must not be selfish any more than your love of me. We will have a chance to talk about this when you come down. (My visit was planned for the first weekend in March.)

February 25 – The retreat so far has been very thought provoking from many a standpoint. The question of celibacy was brought up in this afternoon's conference and discussion period. Many ideas were discussed.

February 26 – <u>Please</u> God, I can love you in marriage at a time as soon as possible, but only when this seems admissable. This is for <u>your</u> sake, and for my sake and our sake. … we made certain promises to one another in the very beginning. Thank God we are keeping them to the best of our ability under the circumstances. The circumstances are trying and I am most certain they will be even more trying. This is not pessimism, but realism. May we be prepared to meet these trials!

(The visit to Washington was wonderful and we were able to discuss the "situation" in person and also to spend time together….. just hanging out.)

March 9 – I really miss you – but I feel that your visit was well worthwhile because we were able to talk about things. It is true that we didn't solve very many problems but I felt very much better after talking them over with you……. I talked with Fr. C. and you scored some points with him …. He thinks that you are mature.* He wanted to know how things went over the weekend. And we talked about some of the same things that you and I talked about…… I really love you and I am more sure than ever. So things are beginning to look better already.

*Roger was 9 years older than me and part of his decision making was his concern that he <u>was</u> older and that perhaps he was too old to start a family and too old for me. I on the other hand thought that I was mature for my age. I had spent a summer during college in Oklahoma doing volunteer work for the Church; I had spent four weeks of the summer after my graduation touring Europe and had worked now for two years teaching high school. I was ready to settle down, be a wife and raise a family. So Fr. C.'s comment was worth mentioning to me.

March 10 – (Comments in this letter refer to an article in the March 12 edition of the Saturday Evening Post about married priests, written by one of Roger's classmates, planning to leave in order to marry.)

Today I had a little chat with the author of the Sat. Eve. Post article. The magazine is sending him all the letters on the article. Most of them are favorable! One nun blasted him. He was a little down in the dumps – guess who cheered him up? Yep, me. His mother wrote him quite a blasting letter after the article. He's going home this weekend to try and straighten things out. They want to interview him on the Mike Wallace show. He isn't interested at the present time. The rumors are flying around here that he is the author of the article, but he definitely does not want to admit it – yet.

So we are not the only ones who are having problems. And though it is going to be difficult, we can work it out. We must be strong and patient.

March 12 – This afternoon Fr. C. and I had quite "a philosophical discussion" of our epic. We did not arrive at any new or startling conclusions.

March 19 – Lots of talk at both the parties about the Saturday Evening Post articles. It's still the big topic of conversation. The way I keep talking, I'll be tipping "our" hand.

(Not too many people knew about our situation; my parents and housemates and a few priest colleagues.)

March 20 – The time is passing – though not quickly enough when we will be reunited – and then the time will pass quickly enough 'til we can really be <u>united</u>. We are both doing well in the perseverance department – I guess it is that we are both stubborn.

However, over the course of these 7 months many things have fallen into place and we will both be the better for it all --- end of philosophizing!

March 22 – I am really looking forward to Easter vacation. It should be wonderful. The happy moments we can have together will make up for the anxiety and the waiting.

There are so many things we have to discuss and so many plans to be made. It will be good to have some time to ourselves.

I don't know for sure but maybe I'll be able to say something to my parents at Easter time. I certainly hope that it will be possible. It would make me feel so much better – so please pray about it.

March 23 – Today I wrote a letter to Kathy* and also one to your parents. Neither letter was very long, but perhaps it said a few things that will help explain "our epic." I hope so. It is so difficult to write things in letters.

Tonight you should be having dinner at home. That's good – you and your Mom will be able to have a good talk.

...... The suffering which we have to endure is a real part of our love. It definitely helps us to grow – it helps us think of one another.

I sure hope that I can tell my parents this time. That definitely is a big bridge to be crossed. If everything is all right at home this time, I think I'll be able to make the crossing. Pray hard.

*My younger sister who was in college.

March 26 – I hope that the letter to Kathy and the one to your parents made some sense to them. I tried to do that. ….. I hope that I will be able to say something to my parents at Easter time; I really believe that this will be a help to us. … We are bound to get a few breaks, aren't we? It seems as if we should be rewarded for our concern for others. Let's hope and pray so.

March 29 – Tomorrow, you will be going over to your mother's and I hope that your visit is pleasant. It will be good to get your parents' reaction to my letter. … News from home is pretty good. It certainly would be nice if I could tell my parents at Easter time. We shall see what develops. …. Last night I had a long talk with Fr. L and Fr. M. about Jacquie and Roger. You seem to be the topic of quite a bit of my conversation and the subject of _all_ my thoughts.

March 30 – I am sorry to hear Fr. L.'s reaction to the Post article, but realistically, this is going to be the reaction of a great many people – probably the majority of people. They kind of "quantify" a person's love of God. This is definitely wrong – no matter who you are or who you are talking about. However, it is not the question here, but it does have overtones……. I love you deeply and I also love God. If you were to interfere with my love of God or if I were to interfere with your love of God, then it would be wrong.... Keep your chin up, and continue to pray hard. More and more we will need the guidance of prayers... don't become too depressed. .....The time is "flying by" in a slow sort of way. It is at least passing, and God is giving us the strength. With God on our side we shall have the only true answer.......it definitely is a terribly complicated world that we are living in.

April 2 – I want so much to make you happy in every way ... Maybe the "worst" is over as far as all the anxiousness is concerned. I certainly hope so. All the suffering has been worth it, because I honestly feel it has deepened our love and this is good. ....God is good, and He has been good to us in many, many ways – mostly because He has given us this gift of love for Him and for one another. There are so many indications that we will <u>always</u> be able to <u>share</u> a life together.

April 3 – I hope that you are feeling better and less depressed. I love you .... Each day I feel more and more confident that things will work out for us.

(Roger was home for Easter and then we drove to Washington and I flew back to Rochester. During the break he spoke with his parents about our "situation.")

April 18 – I just talked to my mother on the hone, and she was a bit upset; I told her that you were here in Washington as she has been trying to reach you by phone. Mom and Dad seemed more relaxed after I talked to them awhile. So with God's help things will work out.

I am sure that your conversations with my mother will be helpful. I told her not to worry, and she said that she would trust my judgment. So things should go a little bit easier in that department. This is one place where I'll definitely rely on your help

April 19 – After I talked to you last night I visited with Fr. C. for about an hour – and brought him up to date. He is going to talk to my mother on Wednesday.

He wonders whether or not waiting a whole year is a very real way of looking at the situation. So many people know about us and it seems like the circle is widening all the while.

I told him that you have signed a contract for next year, and that we had talked about it before you signed. He still thinks we should move the date up – but it seems as if this is what happened before – we moved it up and then back again. With prayer and perseverance I think we could make it through the year all right.

Life with Father

No one more needs to know about us right away, and we can be circumspect about seeing one another, can't we? We have a certain obligation to avoid as much scandal as possible, and I believe we can do this.

Now that we are that much more secure in our love of one another, there are certain things we'll have to bear as much as humanly possible. Certainly our families need a little more preparation – especially my mother and dad because of their age and health.

Fr. C. suggested that I might talk to Bishop Casey* on my way home in June. I'll be giving this some more thought.

*The former Auxiliary Bishop of Rochester, and at this time the newly named Bishop of Patterson, NJ.

April 20 – Fr. C. is going to call and talk to my folks tonight. I hope this helps them a bit. We really ought to double our prayers these days. Yesterday I received the sacrament of penance, and I had a very long talk with the confessor. He promised to pray for us. In parting, he said, "You're honest. God will be good to you."

I really hope that you can "get on" with my parents. That'll make it easier for them. I am also going to write to Fr. V. so he can talk to them.

April 23 – It is almost a week since you returned to Rochester, and with the help of God, things have been going well here. However, I have been a bit worried over what was going to transpire in the next year, but I guess things will work out.

I received a letter from my Mom and she seems to be in better spirits. Fr. C. was going to talk to her the other evening. I am anxious to get his observations.

April 24 – Ours has been a complicated love, mixed up on every side, but we have weathered many a storm already, and we will be ready for the next when it comes.

There can be no doubt about a love that would endure the trials and tribulations we have already endured. And every day I thank you, my love. The hours of prayer, anxiety, counsel and so forth will have their reward. The tremendous wholeness and union we already feel is a certain sign of our love.

Again, what goes before our marriage is well "suffered" because it will make our marital union all the more beautiful.

How grateful I am that you are strong enough to suffer in such silence. It is a tribute to your fortitude and our love. Only God knows what a deep tribute it is.

My sweet, I love you deeply and I want so much to be happy with you, and I believe so strongly that we will be happy. All that has transpired to date is a sign and a good sign of the total happiness that one day will be ours.

April 25 – It sounds as if the girls have a lot of questions for you. And it also sounds as if you have the answers. In a way, these last few weeks of our separation will be the hardest. After that, there will be time to think and plan on a continuing basis. And this will be good. You have been so wonderful through all of this long ordeal and I love you so much for it.

It is so much of a comfort to know and feel your love even at a distance. And I am happy that you can now share so many things with the housemates. I hope your visit with my parents will be productive.

You are so good to think of them and be so considerate. Our happiness I feel will be in proportion to our considerateness of others.

April 26 – Today I received a letter from my Mom in which she sounded worried and upset; so I tried again in a letter to give her assurance that all would be well. I hope your talk with her will help her to be more relaxed.

In your letter you stated how difficult it is for you to go over the whole situation with the girls. I am sorry that it is so difficult, but I guess this is the price we have to pay. This is what makes you so tired and listless. I feel the same way because of the tremendous pressures of it all. I hate for you to have to suffer so much

It is so difficult to understand why our real love should cause so much worry and anxiety. ….. The fact still remains that we have come a long way in these past eight months. …. More and more our love story turns into a greater "epic" each day, and each day our love grows and grows.

April 27 ……. It is so nice that you can come down for four whole days. And I am glad to hear that you are going to take my folks to Horseheads. This will give you some time together, and I am sure this will help a lot.

May 3- We have a lot more than so many other people and so much to be thankful and grateful for … So thank you.

May 4 – Fr. C. and I had a long discussion last evening, and I'll try to communicate a little of what we discussed. We talked of the best way of getting some sort of quasi-official view of my asking for a dispensation from celibacy. So, as it stands not, I am going to write a letter, remaining anonymous, to the sacred Penitentiary which is headquarters for the "internal form" in the Church. C. can mail the letter for me, and receive the response from the Penitentiary. This will give me a chance to put some thoughts down on paper. There have been enough articles written lately about the subject; so I don't need to formally present a "bunch of arguments."

I am merely hoping to find out what the possibilities are at the present time. This will help us in our own planning. ….Remember, my "head is made up!"……. It sounds like you are really getting along fine with my parents. Quis radium. (His slang Latin for hooray)

A thought came to me of late….. What about the possibility of you getting a job teaching at someplace else besides Mercy next year. I know that you would have to be excused from your contract, but maybe at this early date, it would be possible for you to be excused. If we decided to be married before the end of next year, there would be less "scandal" involved.

It seems that there are many things to be decided yet, but in good time, we'll be able to work them out. I am happy in my love of you, and I hope and pray that I can continue to grow in this love.

You have given me so much already, and I know that you have so much more to give and please God, we'll have a life time to share.

Was your evening pleasant last night with my Mom? You will be good for her, I am sure. You're just so good anyway.

May 4 – Keep praying and thinking as we enter phase B of our epic though difficult things will be coming to pass, we will at least be close to one another.

It hardly seems possible that our loved "endured" this year at all. Oh, how much I love you. How much I want to make you happy… I sure am going to try. It grieves me that the circumstances cannot be more ideal.

May 7 – I did call my Mom and we talked things over for a while. She really likes you, and is glad of your help and understanding. ….this morning and throughout the day I took a tour of Montgomery County with my supervisor. It was quite an interesting jaunt. What a contrast – from the very, very rich to the very, very poor.

May 10 – You are sure of me – for I have kept nothing from you, nor could I. As best as I was able, I've tried to share my every emotion – doubt, anxiety, etc. I'll admit that I am emotional, but there is nothing wrong with being emotional – as a matter of fact, it cuts down on ulcers and nervous breakdowns, etc. The "head shrinker's" analysis was that I was emotionally stable – capable of marriage and the priesthood.

(During the past year Roger had visited a psychiatrist for testing, evaluation and consultation to determine if perhaps he had some "issues" which were driving his involvement with me)

In the present set of circumstances, I've had to choose between two goods – the love of you and the love of my priesthood. The love of you has won out! It was not an easy decision to make in view of the "investment" and "satisfaction" I've had in the priesthood.

I have had glory and honors in my "career." From that standpoint, there is nothing wanting. Likewise there is a great amount of security and stability in my present "career." It certainly does not appear that I am running from anything or need to run from anything.

As a mater of fact, I am running toward something – someone. The love that I share with you is a good love, a happy love, a strong love, a growing love, and a constantly fulfilling love. I do not believe that many people (at least from my limited experience) are ever favored with such a love. And I have been around a bit and have some experience from the confessional and counseling in the parlor as well as sundry other experiences.

Because you are the only woman I've ever loved doesn't mean that I love you less. There have been ample opportunities – but I never seriously considered it before.

And this time I've considered it pretty seriously in the midst of a great amount of prayer and study.

Never in my life have I consciously taken advantage of people's emotions, though I've had opportunity enough. This is not in my nature. And I've never felt any need for this sort of thing.

……..A great deal of "ourselves" has already been put on the line, and we are preparing to put more of ourselves on the line as we go along. The decisions we've made already and the ones which we will be making have not been and will not be very easy. One does not make these decisions with anyone. Our love is something special; we are some special people. This is not bragging or complaining; it's merely stating a fact.

I pray daily that I may grow in my love of you and that you may grow in your love of me. So far, our prayers have been answered.

I thank you for all that you have given me and I am gratified for what I have given you.

Please don't be upset because I've reacted "emotionally" to M's ideas – you won't be upset I know. You'll be proud of the reaction – that's why I love 'ya – part of the reason anyway; some of the other reasons: your beauty- both internal and external, your dignity, your intelligence, your sense of humor, your holiness, your selflessness etc, etc.

May 11 – Your letter today seemed much happier – apparently you have been able to communicate more to M. You really can't depend on too many people to be completely understanding from the beginning. If you will remember, we had our own difficulties. …..Your comment about being confident with my parents is well made. See, our "situation" becomes more "normal" as we go along. Thank God for that.

May 16 – When you come down, we can talk this over again and make more immediate plans. Perhaps, it is all too indefinite for you. Even though the time is long to wait, I no longer look at it as being indefinite.
    There are certain things that must be done, and there are certain things we both need to get used to. What we must do is going to take a great amount of courage on both of our parts.
    The time of waiting is also a time of preparation, and as we begin making more preparations, the time will go by more quickly. Jacquie, if I didn't love you so much I would never ask you to go through all of these trials.

And you are capable of going through these trials, I am sure. Once in a while the going looks a little tougher than it is, but that's par for the course.

May 29 – I made arrangements to rent a trailer to cart my junk home.

All the priests will be looking for jobs for me and you. This should be a help. More and more I have my doubts about waiting a full year. In a very real way it seems as if we have suffered a great deal already. After graduation I am going to confront my parents with the possibilities of moving.

This means you will have to think in terms of not going back to Mercy in the Fall. I am not just writing you to upset you, but to try to help you plan. When I call you on Monday, we can talk about it.

I am going to drop a note home now, and you'll be in touch with my folks. So that will be a help to them. It is really great how well everything is going in that "phase." I prayed real hard today at Mass – extra hard!

May 30 – (Roger and some of his priest classmates took a trip to NYC for the holiday. He writes from there) .... This evening we are going to see "Funny Girl." Fr. C. and I talked a bit last night and I felt better afterwards. Fr. S is going out to dinner with us on Saturday when you are here.

June 1 - The NYC jaunt is over and we arrived back safely. It was an enjoyable trip...... It will be just a little while now until Friday – and this will be another milestone. The long period of our separation will have ended.

It sounds as if you have the camp situation pretty well organized. That's great. There are a few problems for me in that department as of now.

IV

An ending and a beginning

I went to Washington in June for Roger's graduation. His parents accompanied me. His Dad had an attack of angina and was in the hospital for a day and missed the ceremony. Mom and I enjoyed the celebration and the festive gatherings with the classmates.

When I arrived Roger told me that he had had an interesting experience just a day or so before. A classmate, a nun, had told him that she needed to talk with him before graduation and parting. She said that she had strong feelings for him and wanted to know if he felt the same. He said that he was so tempted to tell her that he was "taken," but spent some time telling her about his own experience and what he was trying to work out. She wished him the very best. He was struck by the similarity of her need to express her feelings, much like his need months ago.

After the graduation we all returned to Rochester and began to plan our request meeting with the Church authorities. Roger and I met with a monsignor who was the Vicar General. Actually he met with me first and then Roger. During my meeting he tried to persuade me to give up on this situation. He said that Roger was a priest and wanted to stay and that I should leave him alone. When I met with Roger and told him, he was upset and said that was why he wanted to be present at the meeting. He reiterated his love of me and said that he was following the hierarchy and trying to do things "right." Obviously the Church was not cooperating. It seemed as though we were not going to be successful trying to "please everyone."

We continued to prepare for the summer session of camp and I made it known that I was not interested in meeting with anyone else. He would have to do this, since he knew the "bosses" better than I, but I would support whatever he had to do.

He made a trip to New Jersey to meet with Bishop Casey……..his friend and former Auxiliary in Rochester. (arranged by the Bishop)

> Dear Roger,
> I would like very much to talk with you and suggest that Saturday July 9 would be a good day. You could get a plane to Newark and my

Life with Father

chauffeur would meet you there and bring you over to the house and also take you back to the airport the same day.

I am going to Altoona for the installation of Bishop Hogan Tuesday returning late Wednesday night and would suggest you give me a ring about 5:45 p.m.

You are in my prayers. I said a Rosary for you last night. With kindest regards, I am ……..

I thought that I needed a break while he worked out his plans and finalized his decision with the Church. I went to Vermont to visit one of his classmates from CU. Fr. L. was surprised when I arrived without Roger. He thought that we had married and were both coming to visit. I remember that I stayed at the Howard Johnson motel and when Fr. L. came to pick me up, he had to be very discreet, because such a thing could arouse suspicion if someone saw him. We laughed. We had dinner and talked about the events of the last year.

There were eleven classmates in the Social Work program at CU and by the time of graduation all of the classmates were aware of Roger's situation. When he made the information known, he found out that several of them were seriously considering the same move. Fr. L. was one of these.

When I returned to the motel I received a call from Fr. C. who had been in Rochester, helping Roger. The final result of his inquiries through the past few months was that men left the priesthood, married and <u>then</u> filed for dispensation. The Church was very guarded about "ante factum" dispensations. Fr. C. said that Roger had made his decision and had informed the "powers that be" that he would be leaving at the end of summer. Hearing this news, I made plans to leave Vermont the next day and return to Rochester.

When I arrived at the lake I stopped to make a call to Roger and he said he would meet me at my parents' cottage. When we met he told me that he had spoken to the bishop and that he had been told to leave immediately and that he would not be working at camp. It was over. Essentially he had been released of his duties with the diocese and now was on his own. And so we would not wait for a year.

Shortly after this an article appeared in the local paper confirming that "two priests" from the diocese had left the priesthood to marry. Coincidently the other man was the person who had taken Roger's place when he left Horseheads. And the woman he was marrying was a graduate from the same college which I attended. My Dad's comment was that there

Life with Father

must be something in the water at Horseheads! Neither Roger nor the other man commented to the press.

I already had made plans to visit my cousin in Michigan in July and Roger thought that was good and it would give him time with his family and also time to contact Fr. S. and the others about a job. We could then make plans for a wedding and the future.

I visited with my cousin and while I was there received a call from Fr. S. (the one who was not in favor of this 'union' but would support his 'brother') He was in Michigan also visiting some friends and we met for dinner. It was a great evening. He said that he had given Roger some contacts for work in West Virginia. He himself was the new Director for Catholic Charities and was opening an office in Charleston and had made some connections with people at the Welfare Department.

At the end of my visit, Roger flew to Michigan. He had already been to Charleston, checked out the job, which Fr. S. had found, and said that this looked like a good opportunity. He then met my cousins, stayed for a day and returned to Rochester.

When I got home we began plans for a wedding and a move to Charleston, WV. One evening when we were at Roger's home, I mentioned to him that he had never really "proposed" to me. He had told me that he loved me and then we embarked on the long journey of decision-making. The time was perfect for such a statement, because that very afternoon he was talking to his Mom and she had given him a set of wedding rings that she had....not her own set, but an "extra." His mother's birthday was in April (diamond birthstone) and she loved to play bingo at church. She was a frequent winner and had acquired several diamond rings as prizes and likewise had received some as birthday gifts over the years. She was affectionately known as "diamond May." And so on that evening in the living room of his home, I became officially engaged, received the ring and set a date for our wedding…. September 3.

It was already August and so I had many plans to make and had to meet with many people about those plans. The first of those people was my principal-boss at Mercy. I was apprehensive and quite anxious as I sat down in her office. I apologized for having to request that I be released from my contract for the next year. I told her that I would be moving out of state. She asked (to my surprise) if this had anything to do with Fr. Switzer, and I said "yes." Maintaining the dignity and the class that I had always admired in this woman, she simply replied, "Good luck to you

Life with Father

and God bless you." No speeches, no ranting and raving about the Church, she simply asked God to bless me. What class!

My Mom and I began to plan the particulars of the ceremony and dinner for September 3. We went to a local restaurant and made arrangements for a dinner. Roger in the meantime made arrangements with his longtime friend in Horseheads, the District Attorney, to perform the civil ceremony at my parents' home.

I then met with each of my sisters and asked them to 'stand up' for me… be my bridesmaids. Roger's brother, Jerry, the only other surviving Switzer sibling, would be his best man.

I then met with my aunts and uncles. I told them what the situation was, that Roger and I were going to be married in a private ceremony at home and then would have a family dinner at a local restaurant. They would receive an invitation and if they did not want to attend, I would understand. My maternal grandmother (the only surviving grandparent) was delighted about our marriage. She had met Roger when my parents and she had visited DC over Spring break when I was there also. She loved him.

Roger also talked with members of his family, and as might be expected, he met with less than supportive remarks and comments. The two primary people involved were his mother's sister (Aunt Alice) and brother. (Uncle Stewie) No matter how hard he tried, Aunt Alice would not move in her denouncement of him. Finally she told him that if he made this move, he would be 'dead' to her. Stewie on the other hand was more accepting. As previously noted he and Roger were the managers of the 'outfit' and Stewie trusted, believed in and loved Roger dearly. Subsequently he was left to deal with the backlash when we moved to West Virginia. We always kept in touch of course and visited each time we went to Rochester. When Stewie's wife Emma died a year later, he insisted that Roger and I be allowed to attend a small reception at Alice's home after the funeral. She relented. (However she did not talk to her sister or rebuild her relationship until May was on her deathbed. This from a woman who attended Mass daily.)

Mid-August Roger, his parents and I ventured to West Virginia to look for a place to live. We took his parents with us so that they could be acquainted with the territory and feel more at ease about the place where we would be living. We found an apartment and took several jaunts around town.

Prior to this time, I was still living with the girls, but my Mom had asked me to come home for the last week before the wedding, and I did so. It was a good time and it was also easier to be together to make all the arrangements. And now.....everything was ready and of course -----so were we.

September 3, 1966 - the long-awaited day. Fr. C., Fr. S. celebrated the liturgy for the family in the morning in my parents' house. In the afternoon the "judge" performed the ceremony and we were married. Sometime during the day, Fr. C. showed us something that had come in the mail. He kept it until after the ceremony so as not to spoil the moment. It was a picture of a priest saying Mass in Vietnam for the troops, and the sender had written in; "These priests don't have time to date."

Just a reminder that not everyone was happy for us on this day. Actually if it had not been for the previously mentioned news article, there was very little fanfare about this day. We did not seek publicity and tried to be discreet and respectful.

The rest of the day was beautiful. We had the dinner and then we left for our honeymoon trip.......visiting a number of the CU classmates, starting with Fr. L. in Vermont. After a week we returned to Rochester and packed for the trip to West Virginia.

Our Wedding

V

Dealing with the Church (Post Factum)

(the letters that Roger wrote and the responses he received in his attempt to "regularize" our marriage)

On September 15, 1966 Roger wrote the following letter to the Chancellor of the Rochester Diocese concerning his present position.

> Dear George:
>
> Upon my interim visit to Rochester on the ninth and tenth of September, a rumor reached me. According to this rumor, our conversation of August 30th was voided, namely, that the Diocese of Rochester as of now will have nothing to do with my petition for a dispensation from the vow of celibacy

Because I do not want to pay any attention to this rumor, I would like some confirmation from you of my present status. In my last few days in Rochester, nothing was done contrary to what I explained to you on August 30th.

Jacquie and I were married quietly in a civil ceremony at the home of her parents in Pittsford. Only our immediate families were present – twelve people in all. After the ceremony, we had a family dinner at the Green Lantern Inn in Fairport – about 30 people were present. No "display" was made at that time.

Apparently some priest in Rochester calumniated us by spreading stories of a "big celebration flaunting the whole business before the public." May God be good to my clerical brother. The facts, upon investigation, were quite different. Personally, I do not believe the unwanted newspaper publicity helped our last few days in Rochester.

At any rate our departure is history now, and God knows that we tried to be considerate of the Church given the problem of our love for God, one another, the Church and our families strangely juxtaposed by circumstances.

Life with Father

As soon as I hear from you, I will begin the process of formally writing up my petition as we discussed in our last interview. I have already asked John McCafferty to be my advocate. As of this date, I have not contacted the Bishop of Wheeling, but I hope to do so in the very near future. We are trying to maintain anonymity here; my status is known only to my three superiors in the Welfare Department. May God bless the Church in Rochester. Oremus pro invicem. (Let us pray for a resolution)

The response:

Dear Roger:

I want to reassure you that the Diocese will, very definitely, handle your petition for a dispensation from the vow of celibacy so that you can regularize your present status.

John McCafferty has told me that he is willing to act as your procurator and advocate. I know that he will do an exceptionally good job.

As soon as you present your formal petition, I shall send it on to the Holy See and get the necessary authority to set up a tribunal. As I have already told you, I can make no promises regarding time; I can tell you however, that we will do everything that we can here to expedite the process.

With sincere good wishes, I am
Very truly yours,
George Cocuzzi – Chancellor

When we moved to Charleston, West Virginia, the population was about 80,000….. a small city. Roger worked for two months in the job that was "arranged" by Fr. S. Apparently there was some mix-up when he was hired and there was another person hired for the same position. So day after day Roger developed his own job, identifying needs and finding solutions. And he must have been doing it well because soon he applied for the position of Director for the Family Service of Kanawha Valley, and got the job.

Naturally there was some publicity and announcement about a new director. Roger's picture was in the paper and some biographical information was included. " He attended St. Bernard's Seminary etc……" the board who did the hiring was not at all concerned about the details of his situation. They were interested in the job that he could do for them.

Life with Father

November 3, 1966
To Bishop Kearney
 Bishop of Rochester (soon to be replaced by Bishop Sheen)

Your Excellency:
 Enclosed you will find a petition for a dispensation from my vow of celibacy as discussed previously with the chancellor, Msgr. Cocuzzi.
 Your help and prayers are deeply appreciated, and I trust that the solution of my problem will redound to the greater benefit of the Church as a whole.
 Sincerely yours in Christ,

 The Most Holy Father, Pope Paul VI
 Vatican City
 Rome, Italy
 Your Holiness:
 This missive is directed to you for the purpose of humbly petitioning a dispensation from my vow of celibacy. I am a priest of the Roman Tire, validly ordained by the Bishop of Rochester, New York in Americas on June 5, 1959.

I was called to Orders after due thought and consideration by my ecclesiastical superiors. I completed a twelve year course of study at St. Andrew's and St. Bernard's Seminaries in Rochester.

The vow which I professed at the time of my ordination to the subdeaconate was made by me in good faith and after much prayer and thought. At the time, I fully believed that I was capable of fulfilling this vow over a lifetime with the help of God.

There is no reason immediately apparent to me that would make this commitment unlawful at the time it was made. I believe that I was of sound mind, and duly aware of the step I was taking.

However, in the course of my priestly life and ministrations, I have doubted for a long time whether or not the vow was made in my own best interest psychologically. After over a year of study and prayer and counseling, I approached my bishop (in June 1966) for the purpose of asking him to intercede by process for me in an effort to obtain a dispensation from my vow of celibacy.

Several plans were discussed for me to test the validity of this decision. With my consent, it was decided that I should try to continue to function as a priest pending some further action. For two months an effort was made by me to give up an attachment to a particular woman, but this effort failed.

On September 3, 1966, Jacqueline Terhaar, a Catholic, and I were married in a civil ceremony in Rochester, New York. We now live in Charleston, West Virginia. It is my hope that Your Holiness will extend the privilege of a dispensation from my vow so that my marriage to Jacqueline may be regularized. There are no other impediments to our marriage.

It is my hope that some process may be initiated as soon as possible to accomplish this regularization of our marriage.

Briefly I will try to write some of the historical background that has brought me to this course of action. It is most difficult to estimate and describe all of the motivations and emotions which have played a part in this decision.

In the seven years of my priesthood, I have not become disillusioned with my priestly functions or role, but I have found it increasingly difficult to remain mentally celibate even with due recourse to prayer and study. I must hasten to point out that I have not been unhappy as a priest. As a matter of fact I have been very happy as a priest though I have grown more and more unhappy as a celibate. In fear that this was and would eventually block my functioning as a priest, it appeared to my own good judgment that I could best work out my salvation and be effective for the good of the Church outside this priestly role if it meant that I would have to continue to exercise this function only as a celibate. Since in the present economy of the Western Church, a priest may function only as a celibate, I had to come to this choice in conscience.

It is still my hope, though probably only a dream, that some day I can again assume a role as a priest of orders. In the meanwhile, it will be necessary for me to function as a lay priest by reason of my baptismal commitment.

Rather than go into a completely detailed narration of all the steps that have brought me to this decision, may I merely cursorily sketch the details of these past few years.

Immediately after ordination I was appointed by my Bishop to be an assistant pastor in a suburban community of a city about one hundred miles removed from the see city of Rochester. From the beginning, I accepted my duties with a spirit of zeal and enthusiasm for the good of the Church. By prayer and hard work I sincerely attempted to be a promoter of the gospel by word and action. Humanly, it seems, my priestly functions were successful and hopefully I contributed to the growth of the Church, by the grace of God.

After five years in this same parish, the Bishop appointed my to a diocesan position in Catholic Charities. Because of the nature of this position, it was necessary that I pursue graduate studies in the field of social work. For the purpose of these studies I was therefore assigned to do graduate work at the National Catholic School of Social Service at the Catholic University of America in Washington, D.C.

During the first year of my graduate studies, I wrestled with the personal problem of celibacy. Human behavior studies enlightened me deeply. More than ever I began to question the personal decision that I had previously made to be a celibate. It seemed that I had too closely associated celibacy as being totally conjoined to the priesthood.

I know that the Church has always been careful to point out this distinction. However somehow or other in my own mind there was some confusion. This is the crux of the situation, and it seems useless to try to ascertain the complexity of motivations that made me choose to be a celibate. I cannot deny that I was physically free in originally making this decision. Psychologically, the question is less certain.

At any rate, I finished my first year of graduate studies and returned to the diocese. During that summer in my priestly capacity I served as director of our boys' and girls' summer camp. It was during this time that I fell in love with Jacqueline. The future of our love was discussed, and we decided that prayer, study and counseling must be sought as aids to making a proper decision.

When I returned to the University, I began counseling with a particular priest and after some time, with a psychiatrist. The findings of both this priest and the psychiatrist as well as a second psychiatrist might prove of interest when and if some process is instituted.

Briefly, it was the considered judgment of all that I was and had been in sound mind.

Life with Father

Shortly after my sessions with the psychiatrist, I sought and obtained an interview with the Cardinal Archbishop of Baltimore. I had hoped that if I were to present my case to the Church, something might be done about releasing me from my vow before any contract of marriage was entered into by me.

The Cardinal persuaded me that in spite of many things that were being written at the time, there was no hope of the Church listening to my petition. He encouraged me to drop the whole matter. With some resolve, I endeavored to break off my relationship with Jacqueline.

This effort ended in failure on my part. Jacqueline and I continued to write and see each other occasionally. By this time I was well into the second semester of my last year of graduate studies. Counseling with the same priest was continued and another psychiatrist was consulted. When I could not resolve the matter in any other way despite prayer and study, I decided to approach my own Bishop with my intention to seek a dispensation from my vow of celibacy.

The above narrative does not in any way explain the total number of hours of prayer, study and counseling that went into this decision. As a matter of fact it does not present any true canonical case other that I am seeking a privilege in good faith.

I will be most willing to cooperate in any process that can be instituted to give me an opportunity to seek this dispensation in good faith. The wealth of material that has been written about priestly celibacy has given me hope that this petition will be accepted in a favorable light, and I believe that my actions to this date have been honorable though most difficult.

May it please Your Holiness to review this petition in the spirit that it is written. My profession of faith is unaltered. I do not doubt the value of celibacy or the power of the Church to bind or loose me from my commitment. However, may it please Your Holiness to listen to this petition of your humble servant.

The response from Msgr. Cocuzzi (November 8)

I have the petition that you have addressed to the Holy Father for the dispensation you need. I think it will be perfectly satisfactory to have Bishop Kearney send it to the Holy See for permission to conduct the required process.

This is a necessary first step at the present time. In the meantime, I will submit names to the Bishop for the establishment of the tribunal.

As you will recall from my last conversation with you, I cannot give you any indication at all with regard to the time that may elapse between the presentation of the petition and the actual disposition made of it by the Holy See. I can assure you, however, that we will do everything possible to expedite it from this end.

Sincerely yours,

Roger's pastoral experience as the assistant in Horseheads, New York had been wonderful. He was well liked by members of the parish and by the community. Shortly after our move to Charleston, Roger wrote to his former pastor and this is the reply he received. The mention of "Leo" refers to the priest that took Roger's place. Leo left a letter to the pastor and to the Bishop when he left to marry.

Dear Roger:

Thank you for your very kind letter. It was good to hear from you. I appreciate your words and your sincere concern for the Church particularly here in Horseheads.

I have asked the people to close this one chapter in the history of our parish, and this they have done as far as I am concerned. The subject is never brought up….to me. This is difficult. I had such great admiration for you and Leo and so many, many times I want to refer to you for the many things you have done, but prudence tells me: silence.

But the memory will never, never die. I think of both of you so very often. The priests bring up the subject quite often. The priests are confused because they saw in each of you strength and a tremendous future. They certainly had great admiration for both of you. If the giants fall, what hope is there for the rest of us?

If one must leave…. Then Leo's manner of action is more clear to the priests than your manner of action.

I smile now when I think back to the day I had a call from West Virginia telling me of your coming to work there – as a layman. You many be sure I gave the person at the other end of the wire a piece of my mind in starting such a rumor with one of the finest priests the diocese ever brought forth ….. Now I understand.

Well.….. May God have mercy on all of us!

As I said, the memory will never, never, never die. When I expressed to one mother the hope that one of her many sons would enter the seminary, she said. "Oh, so do I ....I guess... but then...I don't know....."

Let us pray...and pray much. God's ways are not our ways. I do not understand my theology, but you may be certain that I am reading much about celibacy and am trying to appreciate positively the gift that I had taken for granted. The positive aspects of the vow are certainly more frequently on the lips of priests.... We are beginning to understand for the first time the power and the beauty which was, in the past, just something we had, but which meant but little to us.

May God bless all of us! These are trying times. Perhaps in the glories of eternity we shall understand.

Gratefully and sincerely in Christ,
B.B.

(How indicative of the Church's way of dealing with an issue.......we will not talk about this. How cruel to the people of that parish who dearly loved Father Switzer. We on the other hand kept in touch with a number of parishioners, and still today, I share cards and visits.)

December 1966

Roger and I went to Rochester to spend Christmas with our families. I was pregnant with our first child. Roger had an appointment with Bishop Sheen, now the Bishop of Rochester. I was visiting my Dad in the hospital. He had suffered a burst aneurysm, and was in recovery. Roger came to the hospital and was irate and disappointed from his visit with the Bishop. Nothing had been done on his case; the Bishop acted like he knew nothing about the situation. He said that he would investigate and continue the process.

Roger's urgency to follow procedure and regularize our marriage waned for a time. He received two letters from Bishop Casey (Patterson) in March and May 1967, mentioning to Roger that he might want to contact Bishop Hodges in Wheeling, and also exchanging pleasantries and prayer intentions.

In January 1969 (we now have two children) Roger writes to Bishop Hodges.

Your Excellency:

> Last Saturday morning Father Leo Lydon called me and said that you were concerned over the fact that my wife, Jacqueline, and I were regularly receiving the Eucharist at our parish church. Father Lydon further stated that you had advised him that he should alert the other

Life with Father

priests in the area of "our situation," and that they should "deny" us the sacraments publicly. He also stated that we would save embarrassment if we did not attempt to approach the Communion table.

We are receiving the Eucharist in good faith, and it is a real sign of our unity with Christ and His Church. Father Lydon indicated that there was "widespread wonderment" over our reception of the Eucharist. We do not believe that there is any "widespread wonderment." Nor do we believe that because some few people are aware of my priestly status that they are likewise aware of the fact that the Church is still censuring our life. To the contrary, we believe that those who know of our situation presume that we have been legally reconciled to the Church; indeed we feel that such is the case, morally speaking.

In spite of the enclosed "official" statements from the Diocese of Rochester, it appears that His Excellency, Bishop Sheen, told me "viva voce" in December 1966 that although he personally did not believe in dispensations, he would see that mine was processed to the previous agreement with the Diocese.

After my visit with Bishop Sheen, I wrote him a note thanking him for his promise to attend to the matter. To this date I have received nothing in writing to the contrary. In May of 1967, I was informed by "one of the officials" of the diocese of Rochester that Bishop Sheen had hidden my petition in the Diocesan Archives. In the meanwhile we have waited and hoped that Bishop Sheen would honor his priestly word in such an important situation.

You are aware, Your Excellency, that similar petitions have been duly processed in much shorter time, and Rome has acted favorably upon them. It seems pointless to go into all of the theological debate about this whole matter. You are aware of the valid theological arguments in our favor.

It is appropriate to mention that the apparent dereliction of duty on the part of Bishop Sheen is now the cause of your dilemma. It is not our intention to be the cause of "widespread wonderment." To the contrary, we have consciously avoided "notoriety."

Enclosed is a copy of my original petition, and I sincerely hope that you will forward this to Rome as quickly as possible. I am sending copies of this letter to the below mentioned members of the hierarchy who are personally aware of this "casus conscientiae." All of these bishops have been consulted in an effort to effect an appropriate solution to the "problem." If the "process" is so important, and if the matter is so "grave," it appears to us that singly and collectively all of these bishops, yourself included, by reason of long time friendship, position of authority and so forth, should see to the appropriate and immediate solution of this "casus." To knowingly and willingly be a partner to the unjust denial of our receiving Christ seems to be entirely not in keeping with the Episcopal role. Should we not be allowed to receive the Eucharist, it can only be construed as an "acceptio personarum."

Your early reply will be deeply appreciated. My wife and I are deeply respected in this community and I am about to assume a position of greater prominence here,* which is a further proof of our "probity of life." Your concern for Christ-like justice is also deeply appreciated.

Fraternally yours in Christ
Roger F. Switzer

*Roger was hired as the Director of Community Council (the planning arm of United Way)

An attempt to explain the delay...... from John Mcafferty – auxiliary Bishop of Rochester

Dear Rog:

Since I saw you earlier this month I have had an opportunity to contact Bishop Sheen. I must say that the past handling of your canonical problem remains as obscure to me as it ever has It seems that just about everyone attributes the long delay to misunderstanding. Very likely this is a factor since you left us at the time of interregnum. (change of authority)

At any rate, I now have it from Bishop Sheen that he is no way opposed to the prompt initiation of the process which we would all like to see undertaken. It seems that I am now pretty much a free agent in preparing any materials needed from the case. I believe that it would not be impossible to initiate the process in Rochester, but it seems to be more customary to undertake it in the newly acquired domicile. I know there is some problem, which has stood in the way of the

Life with Father

process in Wheeling. Will you let me know exactly what the obstacle is – what we can provide to break the logjam?

Bishop McCafferty included good wishes for Roger, me and the children, and also expressed his sympathy over the death of Roger's mother, May..... April 1969.

July 25, 1969 – Roger's response to the missive.
Dear John:

Enclosed is sundry correspondence germane to my "casus." The top letter addressed to Bishop Hodges was <u>never</u> mailed.* Obviously, we thought better of it for one reason or another.

When I talked to Bishop Hodges in June of 1968, he said that he would prefer that Bishop Sheen would release the petition so that he could handle the matter in Wheeling. This I believe I explained to you in July of last year.

When the "furor," described in my letter to Bishop Hodges erupted on Saturday in January of this year, I tried to contact Bishop Hodges by phone. He was unavailable and I talked to one of the vice-chancellors whose name I do not recall. I explained the situation and let it go at that. Bishop Hodges never contacted me and I never mailed the enclosed letter.

Bishop Sheen indeed told me face to face that he would process the case. George Cocuzzi told me that everything was all right in December of 1966. In May of 1967, you investigated the delay and at that time Dennis Hickey told you that bishop Sheen had locked the petition in the Diocesan Archives. This is the situation as plainly as I see it. Thank you for you "intercession" in this matter. Whatever, wherever, and whenever you can do something, it will be appreciated. Thank you very much for your prayers and expression of sympathy at the time of Mom's death. Your presence was a big help to the family.

John McCafferty responded in August 1969, saying he would assume responsibilities for the process, as Bishop Sheen's delegate. He suggested that perhaps a disposition would have to come from two or three knowledgeable witnesses, e.g. the priest advisor and the psychiatrists, and possibly Bishop Sheen himself. August 14, 1969 he wrote that he had received a letter from Bishop Hodges acknowledging

Life with Father

John as the advocate. He also said that it would be necessary for Roger to go to Wheeling to "testify" in person.

The next time anything was "done" on this case was in 1981. We had moved to a smaller community west of Charleston, and Roger was now the Director of the Charleston Housing Authority. We were active members in our Church and our children attended the elementary school.

Roger then wrote to Bishop Hodges and said that he would be available to speak with him (the Bishop) and with our pastor, Fr. S. in Wheeling, when it would be convenient for them.

*The un-mailed letter......Most Reverend and Dear Bishop Hodges

> As the saying goes, this letter is long overdue but it seems the time is ripe as we prepare for Pentecost and all of its implications for us Christians. Hopefully this letter will be one of reconciliation because it needs to be.
>
> In August of 1966 I left the public exercise of my priesthood because of my desire to marry as a step in the process of my own salvation. The agony of this decision has been previously

recanted in my original petition for a dispensation from the vow of celibacy – a copy of this petition is enclosed. I never hear a word (the mail is notoriously slow) from this petition. Your fellow bishops tended to make their own decisions in these matters often times not honoring their previous word. This is difficult to understand and certainly scandalous to say the least. But all of that is history in essence.

There are however, two basic matters that I wish to bring to your attention. One is the regularization of our marriage - at least in the "eyes" of Holy Mother Church we wholeheartedly believe that there has been "ab initio" a "savatio in radice," because of our special circumstances. This seems to be a trouble to you in that you have publicly (at least semi-publicly) defamed us on two occasions in recent years. In my own mind your actions were less than pastoral, but I do not stand in judgment, however, for the public forum, it appears something needs to be done. Do you have a process in mind?

Fr. S will be leaving St. Francis most likely in the next year, and perhaps it would be a good idea to have him actively in the picture during

Life with Father

this process. Fortunately during his tenure we have no doubt about the availability of Christian burial. However this is not as guaranteed, given another pastor or intervention by you in your present frame of mind. In the event of my own death I am terribly concerned over the impact of such a prohibition against Christian burial might have on my survivors. Likewise in the event of my wife Jacquie's death, I would not like the implication of a denial of Christian burial. If you desire, you can most likely clear this matter up immediately.

The second matter is an effort to give you the enclosed publication; <u>Fifty Facts and Insights about Priests Who Marry.</u> Maybe these thoughts will enable you to see another side of our situation. In an effort to clear up the first situation, may I have an interview with you when you come to Charleston for the ordinations? Please specify the time and date and I will be most happy to converse with you.

Sincerely yours in Christ,

Eventually Roger surrendered and gave up the attempt for laicization. His attempts to do the right thing fell on deaf ears…..no one wanted to deal with the issue. In the late 80's Roger consented to be interviewed by the local newspaper concerning the issue of celibacy. People knew that he was an "ex-priest" and they respected his thoughts on the issue. No one ever knew that he did not receive dispensation. It was not an issue within our community. He was a good man, a great husband and a wonderful father. These are the things that mattered.

Scandal to the church community was not an issue for us because the parish we belonged to had issues of its own with which to deal. When we moved into the community in 1973 a new pastor had been assigned. The former pastor left to marry, and one of the former assistants had married the daughter of the woman who married the pastor. The parish was rebuilding.

The issue of Christian burial turned out to be an amusing topic of conversation. In 1990 when Roger died after a year-long struggle with cancer, he was buried at <u>St. Patrick's Cemetery</u>. Furthermore, the then pastor of our parish gave free license to the family for the funeral celebration and a later memorial service. At the latter service Fr. F. gave a eulogy about Roger from seminary and camp days. Fr. F. was now Mr. F. for he too had left the priesthood and married.

After we were married in 1966, the report was that the diocese of Rochester lost one priest a month for the next nine months; included in this number was Roger's former supervisor at Catholic Charities. These were not the "crazies," they were the dedicated, compassionate and caring men who wanted to be married priests.

Within the next few years of our union, ten of the eleven classmates from the Catholic University class of Social Work left the priesthood to marry. Many of them married former "religious" women, nuns. On the occasion of the wedding of Fr. S., I realized that I was the only one in the small group of those celebrating who was not an ex-nun. By this time "leaving" was not an exception.

One issue of scandal surfaced when the pastor of my parents' parish, Fr. R. confronted them one Sunday and asked about our marriage. He hinted that he may have to deny them the Eucharist. My mother replied that it was better for a man to act as Roger did than to hide behavior. (Fr. R was an alcoholic in denial) Subsequently my parents left the parish and joined a neighboring one where the pastor was accepting and could separate my decision from my parents' church association.

VI

Can marriage and the priesthood work?

One man's example and legacy

After Roger died, a friend of ours compiled a book of comments and thoughts about Roger and his work. The testimony of these people is sufficient and valuable evidence that a man can be a priest and be married. The issue is not, as the Church tries to argue, about having enough time to devote to a ministry, it is the person, and who that person is. I also believe that it is important to define "minister." The following excerpts clearly testify that Roger <u>was</u> a minister. His legacy of service and love, which is what he wanted his life to be, lives on in the lives of his friends, colleagues and acquaintances. But more importantly to the issue, it lives on in his children. Roger and I had six children; five boys and one girl. (our sons were named after the priests who had helped us through our "epic," and our daughter was named after our sister-in-law, Ann Marie, who was killed in an automobile accident when I was pregnant with her). Many people have commented to me that that we don't have any doctors, lawyers etc. among them; they are service oriented. Michael is a graphic designer and does pro bono work for community organizations, David and Richard are in education and have served their country in the Middle East as navigators with the Air Guard, Andrew shares his talents with Habitat for Humanity and John (born with Spina Bifida) honors his father by continuing to be independent. Our daughter, Ann Marie was killed in an automobile accident five years after Roger died, and she too served her community well.... and helped her brothers!

And Roger's marriage? He was a wonderful husband. Most of our courtship was by letters, but during some of our face to face conversations we would talk about what our marriage would be like if it ever happened. Roger had a simple "rule" and it worked very well. "We will not compete and we will not keep score."

And so when married, we did not remind one another of how much we did, we did not compare our "jobs." We had the usual share of disagreements and discussions, but as Roger said, jokingly, "I always got my way." I was a stay-at-home mom for sixteen years and I thought it was my job to support my husband in any way that he wanted to "serve." He worked on community projects, church activities and school committees.

We opened our home to help relatives and friends who needed a place to stay, and often we helped other priests who were struggling with a decision, and we took in foster babies. It was when Roger contributed in these capacities that he "ministered" to people.

This is the testimony of his friends and colleagues about that ministry.

We remember Roger................

Roger was the greatest humanitarian I have ever known. Roger was kind, caring, and loving to everyone regardless of race, color, or creed. The Housing Authority residents and staff have lost a friend who can never be replaced. The world has lost a great humanitarian and I have lost someone I truly loved and respected. (manager)

He reached out to mankind. The foundation he prepared will be a monument to the future of all he touched with his wisdom and love. (fellow worker)

His splendid leadership qualities inspired me and others to greater achievements than we believed possible. He wholeheartedly believed in the basic good nature of all people, which sprang, I am sure from his own honest nature. My life has been touched and significantly altered through my association with this extraordinarily kind, gentle and caring man. (his executive assistant)

Roger was one of the most caring, kind and unselfish people that I have had the opportunity to know. He gave so very much in so many ways to his community and will continue to be a shining example for others to follow. (our senator)

Roger gave me a chance to make a better life for myself. I thank God for Roger; he really made an impression on my life and I will always remember him. He was a blessing to the under-privileged. I remember right before Roger passed, we talked about the visions he had that kept him motivated to help the housing community. He said he believed God blessed him with the job so he could help people. When I visited him in the hospital he said, "I believe that my work is done." (former resident)

Roger made a presentation at the Charleston SERRA meeting in which he outlined his hope for the less fortunate people in Kanawha Valley. Roger was then and still remains an inspiration and role model, for me and many others. (friend, fellow parishioner)

Life with Father

Roger was known and respected nationwide. Many housing and social planning specialists urged his impact to their governmental work. He helped localities all over the country; even helped internationally, from the advice he gave me as a member of the U.S. Housing's International Committee. (Housing Commissioner)

To work under the guidance of Roger was a real privilege and a wonderful experience. He was always thoughtful, encouraging and inspiring. (co-worker)

It's just not the same around here without Roger. I miss the way he used to trip on the top step every time he climbed the stairs, the way his hair would stand up on his head some mornings, the way he would always correct my grammar, and the way he would make me laugh with his extraordinary sense of humor. Roger was a true inspiration and a very special person. He gave so much and expected so little in return. I loved him so much and I feel honored to have been called his friend. (executive secretary)

He encouraged ecumenism long before its time. He was truly more than the young assistant at St. Mary's. Roger was the Man of the Year for many years in Horseheads, N.Y. He was the provider, strength, and caregiver for his family (biological) that loved him so. I am truly blessed with many happy memories of

Roger, a man who lived the Christ message, showed it and spread it. How blessed we all are. (nun/friend of the family)

I will always remember Roger as a guy you could trust in everything you ever got involved in with him. Whatever he said, he would do, and do it 100 percent. Simply put, if we all lived our lives the way Roger did, we would have very few problems in this world. (friend and civic leader)

Devoted husband and father; a loyal friend and neighbor; an active member of the Church and school community; an indefatigable worker for social reform as Director of the Charleston Housing Authority; and advocate for the homeless, the poor, the aging. (friend, fellow parishioner)

I will always remember Roger as a thoughtful and kind man. At a time when my heart was heavy with sorrow and pain, he came to me many times with words of comfort. He always assured me that everything would be all right and God was always at my side. (parishioner)

Roger and I were very close, particularly in the last couple years of his life I think we were like magnets. He was such a positive person and I was always on the negative side. He lived the kind of life that could serve as a pattern for everyone. He loved his family, his church, and his life. (friend and parishioner)

Life with Father

We can all learn from individuals such as Roger, for his example transcends all of time. Perhaps, like Roger, we all need a purpose in life; one that is extremely complex, yet as simple as "love thy neighbor and do unto others" without the expectation of any monetary reward – just the gratification of helping and being needed. Roger Switzer – a man for all seasons, a man for all people – may his purpose live through infinity. (school and community friends)

Roger was a very special person, and probably special to many who knew him, because of his wonderful knack of listening without jumping to conclusions. (colleague and friend)

Dorothy Day, Mitch Snyder, Roger Switzer. They all knew what being a Roman Catholic in America was about. What great conversations they are having. (editor of the memory book)

Can a man be a priest and be married? The answer seems obvious. It is not the amount of time one spends with another, but the quality.

Roger was a giving and caring human being, and through his work with the Housing Authority he was able to become a part of people's lives, locally and nationally, and to share their concerns and feelings...... to minister to them. The ultimate tribute to his life of service and love was the dedication of the Switzer

Center, located on the site of one of the family housing developments in 1994. In addition, because of his efforts Charleston now has five high rise developments for the elderly and another family complex.

Perhaps the most touching tribute came to us in a card sent by a nurse who "ministered" to Roger when he was in a local hospital for cancer surgery.

"I had the opportunity to care for Mr. Switzer when he was a patient at Thomas Hospital.

He was one of those rare individuals who had for lack of a better term 'charisma'….. that intangible quality which inspired me as well as others to do their very best without uttering a word.

I know his physical death will leave a great void in all your lives. But he had so much love to give to you and everyone, that his spirit will never die. It will always inspire me and others to give back to the world that love that was so much a part of him."

Breaking ground for the center

Roger & Jacquie at his retirement
September 30, 1990

Presented to Roger for his 20 years of service
to the Housing Authority

Roger F. Switzer

Executive Director

Charleston Housing Authority

April 1 1971 to Spetember 15, 1990

∞∞∞∞∞∞∞∞∞∞∞∞∞∞∞∞

This man

Touched lives And Stirred Dreams

Pointed A Vision Of The Possible

Rolled Up His Sleeves And Built

And Called A Community To Caring

∞∞∞∞∞∞∞∞∞∞∞∞∞∞∞∞

Commissioners Staff And Residents

At His Retirement

Give Love, Recognition, And Thanks

September 30, 1990

Biography

Jacqueline (Jacquie) Switzer was born in Rochester, New York. She attended Catholic elementary and high schools, and graduated from Nazareth College with a BA in Latin. She taught in Rochester for three years before moving to Charleston, West Virginia. Jacquie taught Latin and English in Charleston area public schools for thirteen years. She has a Masters in Industrial Relations and a Masters in Instructional Communications. She is currently an assistant principal in a middle school. Jacquie serves on a number of community boards, was a founder of the WV Center for Dispute Resolution, and is a lector and minister for the sick in her parish. She strives daily to live the ideals that she learned from her late husband.